DOWNLOAD THE AUDIOBOOK FREE!

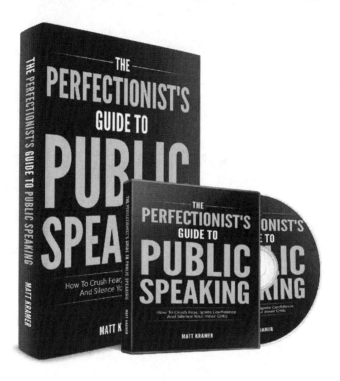

READ THIS FIRST

As a gigantic THANKS for purchasing my book, I'd like to give you the Audiobook version 100% FREE!

Thanks so much!

Go to the Website URL below to get access to the Audiobook:

http://www.tacticaltalks.com/audiobook.html

THE
PERFECTIONIST'S
GUIDE TO
PUBLIC SPEAKING

THE
PERFECTIONIST'S
GUIDE TO
PUBLIC SPEAKING

How To Crush Fear, Ignite Confidence
And Silence Your Inner Critic

MATT KRAMER

Quantity sales. Special discounts are available on quantity purchases. For details, email the publisher at **info@tacticaltalks.com**

Kramer, Matt.

The Perfectionist's Guide To Public Speaking: How To Crush Fear, Ignite Confidence And Silence Your Inner Critic / Matt Kramer

ISBN-10: 1517773393
ISBN-13: 978-1517773397

First Edition

Dedicated to my wife Cindy: The most supportive woman in my life. And come on…did you really expect anything different? She'd kill me if I didn't.

CONTENTS

INTRODUCTION - WHY THE HECK DID I WRITE THIS THING? 1

CHAPTER 1: WHY ON EARTH WOULD ANYONE WANT TO DO THIS? 7

CHAPTER 2: OVERCOMING MENTAL OBSTACLES 11
Trust Yourself 12
Capture What Inspires You 16
Physical Comfort on the Big Day 18
Prepare Yourself 20
Should You Have Notes? 21
The Sound of Musical Motivation 22
Dangerous Comparisons 23
Controlling the Fear 24
      Breathe! 24
      Anxiety Breakers 25
      Distance Yourself 26
      Your Survival System is Not You 27
      Life's Just a Game 28
      Commit and Let Go 28
      Mental Anchor 28
      Remember How Great That Felt? 29
Fear of Forgetting? 30
Shut the JUDGE Up! 33

CHAPTER 3: BATHE IN THE FUNDAMENTALS 37
Entering the Arena 38
From Your Ass to the Stage 39

Show Some Teeth 40

Act the Part 41

Talk with Your Hands 43

Go with Who You Know... 43

Apology Not Accepted... 46

If You Do Forget.. 47

Stage Movement.. 48

Connect with Eye Contact... 50

Turn It Up 51

Diversify Your Vocal Portfolio 52

The Speed of Words... 53

Watch the Clock 54

Deal with It 55

CHAPTER 4: THE BLOOD AND GUTS: SPEECH CONTENT 57

Sculpting Your Speech... 58

Do You Remember Now?.. 60

Start Fast 62

    Tell Me a Story, Daddy 64

    Let Me Ask You Something 64

    What Somebody Else Said 65

    Add a Little Humor to Your Life..................................... 66

    Shock 'Em Dead 69

Structurally Sound 70

Transition Through the Journey 71

Tie Your Main Points to Something...................................... 73

    Story... 74

    Acronym... 74

    Metaphor/Analogy/Simile 74

    Audience Involvement 75

Choose Your Words Carefully 76

Don't Skimp on the Dialogue 79

Don't Fear the...Pause 82

Emotionally Charge Your Message 84
Give Them Eye Candy: Visual Aids 86
The Inevitable Call to Action 89

CHAPTER 5: PRACTICE: THE DISRESPECTED TREASURE 93
How Do You Look on Camera? 94
How Do You Really Sound? 95
Join a Speaking Club 97
Off the Cuff? 98
Fend Off the Filler Words 101
Faces of the Crowd 103
Meet Your Voice 104
Warming-Up Your Voice 106
Practicing Your Speeches 109
Dramatize Your Emotions 112
Seriously, Write It Down 113
Focused Practice 116
Monitor Yourself 117

CONCLUSION – IS IT REALLY OVER? 121

A REQUEST LACKING SHAME 123

REFERENCES 125

ACKNOWLEDGEMENTS 129

ABOUT THE AUTHOR 131

INTRODUCTION

WHY THE HECK DID I WRITE THIS THING?

The meeting was nothing like I had experienced in my entire life. It was a *factory* that produced speakers. There was structure. There was constructive criticism to help make people stronger communicators. And lastly, and thankfully, a supportive group of sincere individuals.

But it wasn't so much who *they were*, but more importantly, who *I was* at that crucial moment.

I know intimately what it's like to be guarded and soft spoken. It wasn't necessarily a conscious choice that I had made to be that way, because as a kid I was plenty rowdy. But as I went through high school I sort of morphed into Mr. Few Words As Possible.

I did nothing but play it safe. I cared too much of what other people thought. I didn't want to make a mistake and I beat the hell out of myself if I did make a mistake—I was a perfectionist. And to top it off, I had no goals. Few ambitions. I mention these embarrassing traits only to give you an idea of where my journey began, because to have any goals or ambitions, I'd have needed to get out of my lobster suit — and at that point in my life, doing so was unimaginable.

The hard reality, I had backed myself into a corner and lived only in that corner. No chances. No mistakes. And of course, nothing to show for it. I thought I was content to do this the rest of my life, but after 26 years, 4 months and 9 days of stagnation, I was convinced that life wasn't about playing it safe. Screw that.

So, with this very group (at the factory) I'll never forget my first time showing up as a guest. I thought I was going to have an anxiety-free, sneak peek while buried in the crowd. Unfortunately, I was wrong. I had to stand up and introduce myself to about 20 strangers, from all walks of life, who now had their eyes *on me*.

Needless to say, from my perspective (and maybe yours), it wasn't without a little bit of heart thumping.

Okay, I introduced myself and *now* I could sit through the rest of the meeting free from participation to see what this speaking stuff is all about — all over, right? Not quite. As a guest I learned that there is a set structure for the meeting (and others like it), which is split into three parts, one of the parts is dedicated to improvisation. This is when speakers get zero time to prepare for a topic that is handed to them right before they must turn and face the crowd. The speaker must offer up whatever the mind can spit out. Imagine yourself in that situation. Yikes.

Here's what happened during that portion of the meeting. Members were being selected at random to go up and speak. I thought to myself, "Man, this looks tough. At least, I won't have to do it."

Or would I?

Understand, the goal of a Toastmasters club meeting (the *factory*) is to make sure that every single member gets an opportunity to speak. And on that night, they did just that. All the members had been used up, and with time still left on the clock, they weren't about to waste it. At that point the conductor began going around the room asking the guests if they wanted to give it a try.

If I thought introducing myself was a pulse raiser, this was like a count-down to death. I was seated on the left side of room and he started asking guests from the right hand side first. You may be thinking that was a good thing for me. But the anticipation, the build-up of nerves, my brain skipping through every possible scenario (with no happy endings by the way) the anxiety built to a point that I thought my heart would erupt inside of my chest.

Also understand that guests are able to decline these *friendly* invitations. But this is something that the very first guest has to do in order to set the tone for the other petrified guests—and by set the tone, I mean to let them know that there's an out! The meeting conductor was already three guests into this exercise and every one of the guests summoned up the courage and did it.

Imagine declining to go up in that situation after all that peer pressure had been inflated to capacity. Here I was pretending to be brave by showing up to this meeting and suddenly there's an opportunity to show just how brave I really am and I was shakin' in my boots. I had wedged myself into a good old-fashioned dilemma—and I was *next*.

As I was waiting in horror for my name to be called, the impromptu segment of the meeting concluded. As in *finished*. Came to an end. Ran out of time. Are you getting this?

Hallelujah! Whew! That was a close one.

As I drove home that night I had a Titanic sized boatload of thinking to do.

Did I really want to subject myself to that kind of emotional trauma? If *almost* being asked to speak was that stressful, what would the actual speaking experience bring? Was it just me who felt like that? Is the benefit or payoff extensive enough to endure so much cardiac trauma? I had a virtual soap opera going on in my head. However, when I got home I knew this was something that I absolutely had to do. I needed the ability to communicate or I'd never be able to present my ideas or be taken seriously. At that moment, I signed the mental contract with myself. I was not turning back.

At the very next meeting, I signed up and became a member. I still had not had a chance to speak in front of the group, but at my third meeting there happened to be enough time available for an additional speaker or two because a scheduled speaker had to cancel. I was asked by one of the club officers if I wanted to, you know, just "get it out of the way" — like an open-mic kind of thing. I thought, "Sure! Can I jab this pen in my eye, too?" Of course, I didn't want to "get *it* out of the way." *I* wanted to get out of there right away.

But I did it. I edged out my fear (just barely) and agreed to speak that night. And I'm grateful that I did. My speech was terrible. Everything about it was terrible. But dammit, I did it. I remember feeling emotionally drained on the drive home that night, yet I also took with me a sense of accomplishment.

That *leap* I had taken was so much more than just speaking in front of a group. It gave me hope that perhaps I could really do incredible things. That I was capable of growing as a person. I must admit, it was a phenomenal feeling.

And if I was able to do it, I knew anyone could do it. Understand that public speaking is a terrifying task to most people, but to a perfectionist there is an added dose of reluctance.

So, let's clarify just what a perfectionist is because, well, that's who the title says this book is for. Primarily, it's one who loathes making mistakes. Perhaps out of fear of looking stupid or foolish. A person that would rather work on and revise something again and again in order to make it "just right," and do this until the end of time, rather than release something that has even the slightest chance of containing an error and thus opening the floodgates for criticism. And if ever there should be an error? Oh boy, watch out because a self-beat down is as guaranteed as the IRS kicking your door down for back taxes.

But, in the case of public speaking, there's an easy solution available to a perfectionist—*avoid it like you would the weird noises coming from your parents' bedroom!*

But something tells me that you've realized, that is *not* a viable option if you want to move forward in your career or excel in life. Look, public speaking is something that comes with a degree of risk. It really puts you out there "naked and afraid" and it won't let you *get dressed* until you *addressed* those risks! A *mistake-hater* must come to terms with this fact.

So this is your book. And here's what I hope you'll gain from it: effective ways to overcome the fear of public speaking, or rather the fear of making mistakes (and the real or perceived consequences of those mistakes). And not only recognize what to do, but learn *how* to do it—this includes how to subdue your inner critic.

A good communicator not only has learned to curb insecurities, ease fear and project confidence, he or she likely uses a number of subtle tricks to mask error and keep on the right mental track. We have those here as well.

As a practical matter, you'll learn how to construct a speech. You'll investigate its structure, learn how to weave your content into your speech and by way of select practice methods, deliver it with all the refinements needed to get your message to stick. Gold for the perfectionist!

My "wake-up" experience with public speaking happened to be in a Toastmasters club, but let me be clear. This book is not intended to be about Toastmasters, nor is Toastmasters a prerequisite to learn or benefit from journeying along with me. I continued (and continue) going to the club and I noticed having a sincere feeling of admiration for all the new members. I knew what they were going through and what kind of courage it took just to make the trip. I found myself drawn to helping and encouraging new members to succeed. And this is why I wrote this book. This is why I want you to succeed. And just maybe, one or two ideas from this book will help you on your journey.

CHAPTER 1

WHY ON EARTH WOULD ANYONE WANT TO DO THIS?

Why should you want to communicate? Do you have ideas? Do you want to share those ideas with others?

How well you convey your ideas will likely determine if those with whom you share them are going to a) understand b) care and better yet, c) do anything about it.

Think about an idea you have been considering. You may be willing to hang out with one or maybe two people and offer your thoughts, but what about five or twenty or one hundred or maybe a thousand or more? Before we continue, grab a napkin and wipe the sweat off this page.

Can you even remember the last time you stood in front of a group of people to say something? Were you a wee bit nervous? Maybe you sang a song using a combination of these beauties: um, uh, ah, err, and "so like"...all so captivating.

Did your heart pound in your chest like King Kong? When you finished, did the crowd applaud because of what you said, or were they just happy it was over? Did you hide behind a lectern or did you wander aimlessly on an open stage? (Trick question, both are sins in public speaking). Did your ability to think clearly vacate when you needed it most? Not to worry, you're not alone. Not by a longshot.

The questions above are all very *dear* to me—because there was a time when my answer to all of them was "damn straight." In fact, I was even called a mumbler by my closest friends and family, including my wife. I countered that they just couldn't hear well. Of course, being called out was hardly a confidence builder. Rather, it only led to further limiting my verbal output.

So let's turn that around. A key benefit of good communication skills is to *build* your confidence!

Have you ever been a bit hesitant walking into a place that was thick with humanity, like a party full of unfamiliar faces or an airport terminal? A place where you could actually feel eyes scrutinizing you more than a TSA body scan.

I think part of that is simple—we care too much about what other people think about us, and the perfectionist in each of us doesn't want to make a slip. Many, of course, might respond to that with, "No, I don't care what they think"—and that's how I may have responded a couple of years ago. However, if you're honest with yourself, you might find the opposite is true.

I would say, instead, that self-confidence or rather the lack of it, is the real reason why we worry about what other people think. Imagine feeling free to prance around and speak your mind, not swallowing your tongue even though you may have a contrary opinion chambered and ready to fire.

If you improve your communication skill set, you will become a more confident person. Not *might*. Will. It's just a question of learning the ropes and then jumping into the ring.

Think about the last time you sat in an audience where someone made a presentation. What did you think of that individual? Whether you enjoyed the presentation or not, weren't you at least impressed with the speaker's ability to get up in front of a crowd of people and deliver a message?

Being able to command a crowd with your words builds credibility. It demonstrates that you know what you're doing and that you're confident doing it. Can you think of any other situations in your life where being able to communicate to your fellow flesh bags would benefit you? What about your job? Your business? City Council meeting? Explaining to a group of detectives that they got the wrong guy? Oh wait, what...?

Moving on.

Obviously, you're motivated and want to learn or you wouldn't be reading these pages. That's wonderful. Your desire is the first hurdle, so you are already well on your way to being that credible individual. Yet, you've really only just cracked open the door. I want you to come all the way. If you master the fundamentals in this book and then go out and put that into action, you will be amazed at your confidence level. You will have conquered what has been said to be the number one fear in life, even above death, and that is *public speaking*. And as a perfectionist, this is a monumental triumph.

CHAPTER 2

OVERCOMING MENTAL OBSTACLES

One of the most repeated bits of advice you'll hear regarding overcoming fear, is to *just do it* — or jump right in and get the experience. And that's a wonderful, tough love piece of advice — yet that only gets you to the party. Even the most seasoned speakers still endure nervousness, which suggests mere experience isn't the end-all for overcoming the fear of speaking. It certainly wasn't for me (a big part of that I attribute to being a *darn* perfectionist).

While absolutely necessary, experience alone doesn't necessarily teach you how to calm the fear, which would allow you to speak more effectively. One of my main motivations for writing this book was this very obstacle. For the first seven months of my speaking journey, my fear never subsided — not one bit. That's when I determined to search out ways to extinguish that fear and then document the methods to see what worked — and what didn't.

Here are several methods that have helped me manage the fear and anxiety associated with public speaking. Experiment. Test them. Find the ones that best work for you. Make no mistake, though, fear is not something that you can completely obliterate (at least not in a short amount of time). But you can *manage* it. You can keep it under control.

Many great speakers that I've studied talk about channeling the anxiety right before they speak, or basically turning that anxiety into enthusiasm or energy that they can then use on stage. There is definitely some validity to this.

Mark Twain has been quoted as saying: "There are only two types of speakers, those that are nervous and those that are liars." While I do understand where Mr. Twain is coming from, I'd much rather kick the nerves entirely. And that's the perspective I want to convey. We want a finished product, but how does one go from timid newcomer to confident communicator?

There have been many books written on just this one subject, yet within those, the minute details and subtle corrections for overcoming fear are rarely highlighted. The only conclusion I can draw is that the authors (hopefully experienced speakers) simply don't remember how it was. As time goes on, the little details—the small personal, mental breakthroughs that inched them forward beyond their fears—were forgotten. So I made it my mission to document these thoughts and feelings while they were still fresh in my mind.

Trust Yourself

The first thing we should expose are the many reasons why fear comes into play. Most people would have no problem talking to their friends in one-on-one situations or even talking to a group of friends. So why is it that we lock up when talking to *an audience*?

Is it because we don't know the people in the crowd like we know our friends? That's maybe tickling the issue. It's actually a variety of things. Do we care too much about what those in the audience will think of us? Will they think we're dumb? And oh golly, what if I make a mistake??? These self-conscious thoughts may dominate our minds. When we think too much about the "what if's," it only puts more pressure on us. That's not good.

So what *is* the solution? There isn't just one; there are many. And they constantly change and evolve as one gains experience.

Here's a great place to start. If you did nothing else but this, you'd be well on your way to becoming a capable communicator: Build up your confidence! But let's be real. This isn't something you can generate in colossal abundance moments before you get on stage. Instead, it's something you should be working on every single day of your life.

Come to terms with who you are and accept yourself. Sounds like a therapy session, right? Think about it, if we were comfortable in our own shoes then we wouldn't be thinking about the "what if's," they simply wouldn't matter. The goal then is to stop worrying about what everyone else may or may not think about you.

One method that has worked particularly well for me is to visualize. For example, imagine yourself right now in a full suit of armor like Iron Man, the cartoon version or Robert Downey Jr., whichever, doesn't matter. Then imagine being surrounded by people that are hurling the most obscene or demeaning insults in your direction. While those vile missiles might be aimed at your tender, insecure spots, instead, imagine they now hit your armor falling harmlessly to the floor.

So, put on a smile while this is going on. Look at their faces, wish them the best as they tire realizing their railing is pointless. No need to say anything back to them in retaliation, just smile back. Pretty cool, right? If you didn't do it, you've got 30 seconds to do so or this book will self-destruct. 30, 29, 28, 27, 26...seriously.

If you are reluctant to attempt the exercise above, I completely understand. I used to think visualizations were a steaming pile of feces. But, after trying them for myself in various situations, I am a believer. So don't do as I did and wait years to give the method a chance. Yeah. Visualizations. Write it down. Use them.

Next, from the book *The Four Agreements* by Don Miguel Ruiz, heed the second [agreement] and don't take anything personally. I'm sure you've heard that before — yet it's not an easy task. But Ruiz explains that whatever someone else says or does, has nothing to do with you. Everyone sees the world from a different perspective with different standards they live up to — or agreements — as described in his book.

We judge everyone else based on the personal standards that we hold for ourselves. So when someone tries to put you down, they are really trying to hold you to standards that they have agreed to in their own minds, and in most cases ones even they can't live up to.

This is powerful. If you can understand and internalize that agreement, you'll go far. Nothing anyone else could say or do would be able to affect you. This is another technique to work on daily because typically we've been conditioned to worry about what other people think about us. That really limits us as individuals.

Here are examples of the things you can do daily to help break the self-conscious hocus-pocus.

- Speak up in places where there are people. In a check-out line for example, instead of trying to talk quietly and directed towards the cashier, speak louder as if you didn't care if the people around you heard. Even at the risk of being obnoxious.
- Drive with your windows down and sing to your heart's desire. We all sing when we hit that lonely stretch of highway anyhow, so why disrupt the beauty just because cars are right next to us?
- Be more animated or enthusiastic with your voice and movements when talking to strangers, almost flamboyant. It's for a good cause.
- Go out of your way to make eye contact and smile with complete strangers. If they don't smile back, no worries.

This sounds incredibly silly. I get that. Yet remember, this worrying about what others think is a big part of where our fears originate, and by doing things that stretch your comfort zone you are investing in yourself.

The idea is to do the things that your mind is apprehensive about doing, whatever that may be for you. You might very well be comfortable screaming at the top of your lungs in your car, at a stop light and with the windows down. You know yourself better than anyone, so listen to your mind during the day. It will tell you when an "expanding" opportunity arises because it'll try to pull you back to safety. At that moment is precisely when you take over and say, "Not so fast!" and proceed to do the opposite.

Your makeover won't happen overnight. It took years to build these tendencies, so don't expect them to be gone in a couple of attempts. You need to keep stretching yourself little by little, and over time you will see a huge difference.

Capture What Inspires You

This one continues to amaze. Carry around a small note-book and jot down new "Aha" ideas or bits of inspiration. You never know when something will click in your head and give you a clear perspective on something, so you have to be ready.

For example, maybe you wake up one day with a certain inspirational feeling that helps you think clearly about something that troubled you the night before. Write it down—now. Our minds are constantly sifting ideas, moving them in and out of our consciousness. Get those ideas recorded before they disappear. Because they will if you don't.

You may be saying to yourself, "That's a great idea! But wait a minute, what does this have to do with overcoming my fear of public speaking?" Let me explain.

We aren't robots. We can't flip a switch on our circuit board and set our mood to "Positive Mental Attitude – 24/7." Not possible. On the other hand, it seems *negativity is* all around us 24/7. Have you watched the news lately? You can't miss its negative tone. Topics such as theft, corruption, war, kidnapping—the most hideous things imaginable capture our attention.

And in case you don't own a TV, more of the same is also broadcast through the newspaper, the internet, friends and family who *do* happen to have a TV. Heck, you even hear it at the gas pump! Then on every corner, it seems, we find those who have made it their mission in life to bring down others, preferring mediocrity over excellence—that includes our own internal critics.

You can't let that seize you. It touches us all, but when you get to the stage, you must be insulated. It's not easy to shield our minds from infiltration by these negative combatants, but awareness of those issues (and some positive tools and techniques on your side) can win the day.

In case you're still struggling to find the correlation between general negativity in life and defeating the fear of public speaking, let me just say this…they are very much related.

The inspirational thoughts that you scribble down are meant to keep you fighting on through tough times, to motivate you to overcome the negative thoughts that occupy your mind. It's easy to want to quit (almost the default reaction) when the going gets tough. The "going" in this case is public speaking, and the "tough" is the fear and all its associates (physical sensations, mental warfare, self-criticism, and whatever else our clever perfectionist minds might whip up).

And when the thought of standing in front of an audience gets you to the point of asking, "Why the heck am I doing this?" just pause. Pause and consider some of those inspirational thoughts you've logged. They are strong medicine. They're your espresso shots. Your fuel. Maybe even that bucket of ice water dumped on your reclining soul in the moments before sleep.

Now that we know their purpose, let's get back to capturing those inspirational thoughts.

On the matter of what others may think of me, for example, the thought came to me: *No one is going to live my life for me.* Those people doing the criticizing, or the dream crushers as I like to think of them, were NOT going to live my life for me. They weren't going to go out and earn a living for my family and me. So why would I allow myself to be dragged down? I wrote it down and by doing that I locked in both the inspirational thought and the context it addressed.

This mental breakthrough that I wrote down was for the perfectionist within me:

There is no such thing as perfect.
It's okay to make mistakes.
If you do make a mistake, don't beat yourself up.
Stop being careful and set yourself free.
Be yourself, trust yourself.
Enjoy the journey.

That had an enormous, positive effect on my overall way of thinking when I initially jotted it down. In fact, it still does.

When I would feel the urge to stay home instead of going to a Toastmasters meeting or another opportunity for growth, I'd flip through the pages of my notebook to this gem: *Comfort makes cowards of us all. It can seize us when we're least expecting it.*

You get the idea of the kind of things to be on the lookout for. Continue adding to your notebook and go over those entries on a regular basis. The wonderful thing about having these in a small notebook is that you can carry it on your person. You can bring it with you when you're scheduled to speak, inspirational thoughts, accessible right before your presentation.

Physical Comfort on the Big Day

The previous steps were really about building one's own personal confidence, or personal power. The following is going to layout actual techniques that you can apply on the day you're set to walk to the podium.

Above all, make sure you have enough energy to give it your all. This means getting enough sleep the night before, which may not be so easy, especially if your mind is focused on your presentation for the following day. A full night's sleep is the goal, but if that's not possible, a 20-minute power nap an hour or two before you leave the house can re-energize your mind.

Don't arrive on an empty stomach, neither having just stuffed yourself like a Thanksgiving turkey. The consensus is to eat an hour and a half to two hours before you're set to present. And then these:

- Drink water and stay hydrated. Light meals such as chicken, unsalted almonds or other nuts, fish, egg whites, and rice.
- No caffeine (if you are sensitive to its effect), no alcohol, no spicy food (unless you can speak from a toilet), no yogurt or dairy products because they clog up your throat, avoid new exotic foods that you've never tried, you get the idea...

Feel free to experiment for yourself. Your goal is to feel great physically because you'll need the energy to fight the real battle against your nerves.

An important thing to mention here as well is the debilitating "cotton mouth" — where you get so dry it severely inhibits your ability to speak. Of this I thought initially it was due to speaking for long periods of time, so I began bringing water and monitoring the types of foods I ate beforehand. I would even avoid brushing my teeth within two hours of when I was slated to speak, thinking that the film coating from the toothpaste may have been the culprit.

However, even after taking that action I noticed it persisted. During one speech I gave in Toastmasters, "dry mouth" got so bad that I could barely finish a sentence without making contorted faces in an attempt lubricate the inside of my mouth. I was doing everything I could to try and produce spit, but none came.

That's when I discovered a simple truth. The condition was a direct result of anxiety. During my speech evaluation that night, an experienced member gave me advice and explained that cotton mouth was due to nervousness. She also said to bring water up to the stage and to take a water break during the speech if necessary. (Helpful advice). Ultimately though, as fear is put in check, so goes the cotton mouth.

Additionally, the clothing you wear can also play a role in how you feel and your level of confidence. Some outfits make us feel better than others, plain and simple. I have a simple criteria for this: Dress in comfortable clothes that you can move around in *and* that make you feel good about yourself.

In terms of appearance, a rule of the fat finger is to dress similarly to the audience—but one step above. It's not a bad rule to go by, still, I'm not much of a full suit and tie kind of guy. In those cases I'd pick the sharpest, though still comfortable (to you) outfit.

Prepare Yourself

Another key factor involved in building confidence and alleviating stage fright—both in outward appearance and internally—is how well one knows the material. If you've prepared well and know your material thoroughly, you will be much more confident than if you didn't. As perfectionists we tend to over-prepare, but for the ulterior purpose—to avoid that dreaded mistake.

On the practical, tactical level, knowing your material well means you are never far from a key "landmark." That is, if you get lost midway through your speech you are still in the game. While you may need to improvise a moment to buy time to find your place, if you have prepared mentally for that situation (and it happens to all speakers) you can keep your hand off the panic button.

Of course, the subject matter can make preparation much easier. Are you talking about something you truly know and care about? You should be. Topics can range from an enjoyable hobby to information about your industry or profession, to an array of personal experiences.

When you stray from this realm and lack authenticity, surely you will lose your audience. They want the truth, the whole truth, and nothing but the truth.

The benefit of talking about something you are excited and passionate about is that those qualities shine through. Passion is contagious so let it work for you. I say, infect the entire audience.

Should You Have Notes?

Peace of mind may also have a soothing effect on your nerves. Fear of forgetting material was a real problem for me, especially since that whole perfectionist *thing*. One way to quell this concern is to have notes in your back pocket or somewhere on your person. If you have a lectern, stool, or table, use it to your advantage to place your notes there along with a water bottle. To be clear, ideally, you want to avoid using your notes. Yet, in my experience, just knowing they're there has given me a clear confidence boost. The perfect safety net, if I do get lost, they're there for me to glance at and continue on.

In fact, I witnessed a seasoned veteran of Toastmasters and keynote speaker, on multiple occasions, reach into his pocket, glance at his notes, and continue on. He even flat out told us as he was digging in his suit pocket for the notes that he had observed an admired speaker of his do the same. "Why not him, too?" he said. Touché.

There's more to that, of course. A lot of what you can get away with on stage comes down to how confident you are while doing it. I'd estimate one could stop mid-sentence, walk over to a microwave, pop in a frozen burrito, and resume speaking from where he or she left off without a peep from the audience—if they believed in the speaker.

So, should you have notes? I think so.

The Sound of Musical Motivation

Music matters. This may be a familiar concept to you, but I absolutely must include it. Before you're set to speak, listen to music that pumps you up, that makes you feel confident, motivated, even focused.

I like a lot of different types yet that doesn't mean all of it motivates me. My preference for this purpose are songs that have no lyrics. Yours might, though, and that's okay.

You want to listen to *your tunes*. We all have different tastes so we aren't limited to a single genre. I enjoy Native American flute and Celtic music. They help clear my mind and prepare me for battle. I mean *really* prepare me for battle, like on the set of Braveheart. No, I don't picture an actual battle scene, but rather mentally prepare for one as if I were marching to the front.

The intent of your battle tunes is to calm down your thoughts and put you in a motivated and confident state. They may not always accomplish all, however if part of the music mission is met, it is certainly better than none.

Music, like inspirational thoughts, gives you a perspective, and sometimes it's hard to replicate an exact state of mind that a song may have encouraged in the past. Sometimes it loses its novelty or sometimes you're just too riled up.

Think of a song that you've worn out because you've heard it too many times—what was once amazing to your ears is now a thing of the past. Keep this in mind when you find a song that motivates you. Save the song for this very purpose to extend its motivational life instead of draining all its juice in one day. For example, have a song that is exclusively for your speech preparation.

Break out your boom box before your next presentation and get pumped!

Dangerous Comparisons

Do you have any role models in the speaking realm? Those to whose level you aspire? As a beginning speaker, there is a good chance that you'll encounter a lot of speakers that tower over you in experience and skills. There are two ways to look at this. You can have a healthy admiration for someone whose skills are elevated and use them as motivation to reach that level. Or, you can become discouraged by the noticeable gap between where you are, and where they are.

To avoid the latter, don't compare yourself to anyone else...at all.

In a similar vein, for example, perhaps you're in a position where the speaker before you is a speaking connoisseur who blows the roof off the building and drops your jaw on the floor. When it's your turn, that inevitable comparison could take your focus away from your own message. And if you're a beginner, get ready for a long night. My advice? Don't torture yourself.

You are who you are. Keep your focus on you *and your progress* rather than someone else and where they are in their journey. We each learn at our own pace, it's as simple as that. But simple doesn't mean easy. It's hard not to want to be great in the quickest way possible. Unfortunately, any desire to shortcut the process may only hinder your progress.

You must go at your own pace and block out the urge to compare yourself to others. If they excel, it only means that they've been at it longer than you. No problem. You're on your own journey and you'll get there when you get there. Take comfort in that.

Controlling the Fear

Now for the "fun stuff." You're waiting to be introduced and your mind starts to wander to all the places you don't want it to go with the negative "what-ifs". This may be the toughest part about getting in front of people and sharing your thoughts and ideas, a place where I really struggled.

At one point, I felt like it was getting worse with each speaking opportunity and that produced a feeling of hopelessness. Specifically, I had to deal with nerves, my heart beating off the charts, and to top it off, my mind would play out all of the scenarios where I'd fail miserably. As you might imagine, all of those obstacles affected my energy, enthusiasm and, more importantly, my confidence—everything I needed on stage!

But I would not give up. After all, I had already scratched my way through the initial barrier—had actually stood in front of a group to speak. So what next? The following have worked and continue to work for me.

Breathe!

The first thing you should do is *breathe*. Take a deep breath in through your nose, hold it for 3 or 4 seconds, and then exhale through your mouth. Do this several times to help relax your body. Feel the tension all over your body and just *let it go*. A good way to do this is as soon as you exhale, let your shoulders drop and your muscles disengage. Relieving this tension will make it easier to mentally engage these ensuing techniques.

Understand that it's not just you who experiences feelings of anxiety. These wretched feelings abound with virtually every speaker at one time or another and are completely normal. Dismiss that "why does this have to happen to me?" babble because it only dims your focus on the task at hand.

Anxiety Breakers

So, put the entire situation into perspective with a couple of anxiety breakers. For one, you are *not* in any physical danger. You're not about to be eaten by a grizzly bear or engaged in a firefight. Your being is simply reacting to thoughts. Even though logic is a hard sell when nervous, this particular rationale has been very effective for me.

And another, recognize that thoughts aren't real unless you let yourself believe they are. They are electrical impulses in your brain popping off in rapid succession like a strip of Black Cat fireworks. We tend to overestimate the gravity of these mini-explosions and turn them into nuclear blasts.

Can you remember a situation where you imagined that the worst possible outcome was inevitable, but then you ended up being completely wrong? Or, what about the assumptions that we make on a daily basis? Here's an example. My wife ran into an old friend from high school one time at the store and she made the risky assumption that her friend was pregnant. She said to her *friend,* "You're pregnant again?" She wasn't.

My wife even had the help of visuals (her friend's waistline) and yet she was still led astray by her preconceived notions. Our brains are big fat liars sometimes as the cerebrum tries to determine facts before collecting all the data — knowing this tendency can lessen the impact of our overblown thoughts with regards to fear.

Distance Yourself

Distance yourself from negative thoughts when you sense them poking at your consciousness. What I mean is to *separate them* from you. They aren't you. Treat them as if you were merely observing them. For example: "Oh, that's interesting. Negative thoughts are present." or "Very weird, my body is acting as if I were in real danger."

Try putting some "funny" in these observations as well such as, "Incredible, my inner critic is trying to put me down to make himself feel better. What a silly fellow."

Turning tense moments into mere observations gives you a unique control over them.

There have even been studies on how labeling emotions, or *affect labeling*, can actually lower the emotion's overall effect on you. One study in particular, headed by Neuroscientist Matthew Lieberman, an associate professor at UCLA, describes how affect labeling can disrupt the response of the amygdala—thought to be part of the limbic system within the brain, which is responsible for emotions, survival instincts and memory. Basically, by labeling your emotions, you disrupt the amygdala, which is what allows you to perceive emotion.

Limbic what? Amygdala? Yeah. I didn't take that class either. Okay, it's like if you were watching a horror flick and during a hair-raising scene I come and stand between you and the screen, which blocks your view of the creepy. The scene would probably lose some of its edge, don't you think?

It's also a common teaching of meditation practitioners to observe one's thoughts and label them during meditation. It's done as a means to raise awareness to a particular thought or emotion, which is particularly helpful if you intend on changing your thought patterns toward fear.

When I distance myself from emotions and negative thoughts in that manner, they sort of disappear. It's as if they could only affect me if I were oblivious to them — but I'm onto them!

Let's not be naive here. There is a wide variety of negative thoughts and emotions that attack simultaneously, and each of us have our own thin spots in the wall of confidence. Still, you really have to work on addressing all emotional assailants (or at least the dominant ones).

Your Survival System is Not You

The body's survival system doesn't understand the difference between real or imagined threats, and so it acts accordingly. Call it a fight or flight response, even though there is no physical danger. I try to distance myself from my body's survival system in that when I sense it activating, I'll understand that it's just trying to protect me from perceived danger.

Example: "Oh, how cute. My body's survival system is engaged. It thinks I'm actually in some sort of danger."

Don't get frustrated that this occurs, survival mode is a default mechanism. Do your best to put it in a positive light and just be grateful it really works! I want mine fully functional in a moment of danger rather than being so calm I don't think to move from the path of an oncoming car! This technique helps lower its overall grasp on me.

An added yet incredibly important note about not getting frustrated. Embrace the fear. Hug it. Love it. Accept it. When any (though possibly varied) reaction to fear manifests itself, accept it right away as normal. Heart beating off the charts? Get excited! That tickling of the solar plexus (butterflies in your stomach)? Smile and laugh inwardly. Incredibly effective.

Life's Just a Game

Add to that this little tip. When it comes to public speaking, this should be in every perfectionist's toolbox. Picture life as just a game. Yes. Because it's just a game, there's no fear of failing. You can relax in total freedom from responsibility, free to perform to the best of your ability.

Commit and Let Go

And then there's this gem: let go of the outcome and fully commit. By commit I mean that you tell yourself, "I'm doing this. I want this. I choose to do this." And mean it! The commitment gives you a place to focus your remaining nervous energy and the sooner the commitment, the less impact from nerves. And, let's not forget—no one is forcing you to advance your speaking skills. This is your choice, with extra emphasis on the word YOUR. You don't have to be perfect. Being yourself is sufficient. Do your best and let the pieces fall where they fall.

Mental Anchor

Another element to have at your disposal is a "mental anchor." Mental, not metal. Find something that you can use to keep your emotions anchored to reality. Just a thought that will put things into perspective for you—and do it quickly. Mine was simple. I'd look around the room prior to speaking, usually right when I noticed my heart pumping faster than normal and think: "It's just a room—with people—and all that I'll be doing is talking to them."

Your anchor could be something completely unrelated to speaking. For example, telling yourself that you're only human. Perhaps this can alleviate some of the pressure you've put on yourself to wow everyone in the audience.

It could also be a person, place, or thing that's important in your life. If you have a spouse, kids, business, a goal, or whatever has meaning to you, use it as an anchor. Focus on the reality of those things. And the reality is, they will remain important regardless of whether or not you trip over your words in the middle of a speech.

An anchor can even be the poster boy for what an anchor is supposed to do under this circumstance — remain calm and cool under stress. Who's the poster boy you ask? *Cactus.* No matter if it's scorching hot in the summer or a flash snowstorm blankets them in ice, those suckers go about their business unfazed. Simply visualize a cactus under extreme weather conditions; see how it endures the worst. Just as you will.

Whatever your anchor happens to be, its purpose is to keep your emotions and your thoughts in check, neither too high, nor too low.

Remember How Great That Felt?

When you've got your nerves at a manageable level, it's time to enlist your emotions in your behalf. For example, think back to a time when you achieved something or did something successfully that you were excited about. Did you get an award? Win a competition? Score the winning run? The "what" doesn't matter, but rather it's those emotions you experienced.

Try to put yourself back into that very state of mind. This method works well in two ways. One, it puts you in a more positive mindset, and two, it distracts your conscious mind from errant, negative thoughts.

As an aside, from this day forward when you experience happiness or proud moments, bottle those feelings up. Try to lock in every sensation so that you can reuse them over and over again.

The tips that we've gone over for *controlling the fear* can serve as a checklist you can run through in your mind as you're waiting to speak. But don't think you'll need to use them all, every time. Chances are you will find that two or three of these techniques work best for you and you'll end up using those.

Still, you must start by *breathing*. It's not optional. Like seriously — you'll die if you don't. But in this case, be sure to take deep breaths. This is a mechanical means to calm your body down which will allow you to move through this "checklist." Believe me, you'll be glad you did.

Fear of Forgetting?

Forgetting. This one is high on the to-*not*-do list for us perfectionists. Doesn't it make sense though? If the top fear is that of making a mistake and looking stupid, forgetting what to say is right there with losing your lunch, or finding out a body cavity search is imminent. Ouch.

The good news is that we're wrong in our assessment (at least, the forgetting part) of this potential scenario. It's only our fears talking. Everyone forgets things at times, it's a normal human experience. Still, I'm not naive enough to believe this isn't a serious concern for most perfectionists. It certainly was for me.

So then, it's important to avoid thinking about making a mistake during your presentation, in particular, "What if I forget what I'm going to say?" If your mind fixes on that, chances are you *will* forget. You don't need to stack the odds against you.

If effective public speaking were a superhero, then its arch nemesis would be the mid speech white-out. When the mind goes blank, it goes blank. Bye-bye to your thoughts —

especially any cohesive ones. And when it goes during your speech, you no longer have the ability to think or remember what the heck you were saying. It's like you mistakenly hit the reset button on your calculator.

The following is how I can best describe what happens. There's a sudden feeling of "Now, where was I?" followed by the realization that you are still in front of a crowd staring and waiting for you to continue. Then comes the brain scan where you try as fast as you can to remember where you left off in your speech. When it doesn't come, panic does.

It was one of my ultimate worries starting out and during my second speech in Toastmasters, it came out to play.

Everything was going great—right up until the 30-second mark of my speech. Then, as the last sentence poured out of my mouth, it hit me like a grenade. I knew instantly that I was lost. I couldn't remember *jack*. Not even a basic idea of what I was talking about. I performed a quick brain scan, but nothing showed up.

At that point, I looked at the floor just hoping that the words would come. But they didn't, so I pulled out my speech notes from my back pocket. It was going to be all right—but then it wasn't.

My notes consisted of a few bullet points scribbled onto a folded index card. I gave them a good look over as if they were helping, but inside it was, "Oh crap." I slid my lifeline back into my pocket and got back to my bread and butter— intense thinking.

You see, there wasn't anything wrong with my notes. They were written exactly how they should have been. Some trigger words for the introduction, some bullets listing the main points, and some more trigger words for the conclusion. The trigger words were supposed to jog my memory, but they didn't. And the reason they didn't is, unfortunately,

I memorized my speech word for word (a matter I'll get into later).

I began apologizing to the audience as I paced back and forth a few times, head facing down to the floor, cringing inside. I tried to hold back my frustration with myself, attempting to cover it with a smile, but it shone through. I even reached for my back pocket again, but stopped short, recalling its futility (at least I remembered *something*).

In real time, this entire ordeal lasted 24 seconds. It weighed much more.

Finally, perhaps out of sheer frustration, I began muttering some words, basically repeating what I had already said, just in fewer words. It helped. I latched onto my speech trail and continued on. Once I got going, I made it all the way through. It was as though I'd experienced the worst and now the pressure was off allowing me to get through it without another silent sermon. I was just glad to have finished it, however, from my evaluation later, I learned I still wore the visible frustration on my face. It was not a clean escape.

Yet, I learned a lot from that experience as in, why did this happen? I attribute it to several things I did wrong. I memorized my speech word for word, and then went out and proved that nervousness and memorization aren't a good mix.

Also, as I explained previously, I was too concerned with the "what-ifs." Mental preparation and an understanding and internalization of the fact that it's truly okay to make mistakes is crucial. These tactics help take the focus off the dreadful "what-ifs" so once your mind is no longer focused on them, going blank isn't a big deal. I've yet to lose my place mid-speech ever since, well, at least not with the audience knowing I did. (Cue the laughter: Muahahaha).

These techniques tipped the scale in my favor for overcoming and controlling my fear of public speaking. And that control has continued to grow. Maybe it's at about 91.7 percent control for me, 8.3 percent fear. Something like that. Flip flop those percentages and you get a charitable figure of where I started. I am just grateful it's possible to diminish one's fear of public speaking; it's just about finding what works for you. It's about finding your own special formula.

Shut the JUDGE Up!

This part is crucial, my fellow perfectionist, so read with eyes wide open. We must throttle the internal critic (our Judge Dread or however we view it). And if you can't do that, you must at least hone your ability to ignore it. If we don't, the judge will chain us down and prevent us from improving.

First off, after every speaking opportunity, remind yourself what a good job you did getting up there and doing it! If you made a mistake such as forgetting an important point, jumbling your words, or whatever, let it go. Try not to beat yourself up. This is such an important part of the equation because if you're hard on yourself for making a mistake, then you'll only strengthen the fear of making the same mistake next time. The idea is to improve, not to hold yourself back.

The mere fact that you got up there to do it is a strong step and you shouldn't let it go unnoticed. Make it a point to find the good out of any speaking experience, no matter how miniscule. Our *judge* will find something to latch onto (a mistake) and try to slap us in the face with it. Things such as, "I can't believe I forgot to say that," or "I'm so stupid for mispronouncing that word," or "The audience hated it, they looked so bored," or "Why can't I just deliver my speech perfectly without making mistakes?" are hard to shake. We must ignore that *conniving bastard*. Each time you sense a negative thought arise, cover it by telling yourself something good that you did during your speech. You always have the comfort of knowing you, at least, showed up, *right?* That's not always the easiest thing to do, so it's always worth noting!

Of course, this doesn't mean pretending there is no need for improvement. As blissful as ignorance would be, your goal should be to improve, so simply telling yourself "good job" is not enough. Honest self-analysis should point you toward working on the things you want to improve for next time. The intent of the healthy self-analysis is to allow yourself to grow and develop into a better speaker. On the contrary, the internal judge's criticism seems intent on doing damage by infecting your mind with self-doubt. You don't want that.

And, despite your own (critic's) disappointment, you should also listen to the people that support you. Don't fight their words of encouragement. When your spouse or a friend tells you "Good job," accept it and be grateful. Encouragement is important to keep you going forward, especially for something as nerve-racking as public speaking. Sure, there is some possibility of being trapped by hearing all praise and no criticism. On the other hand, what possible benefit could come if you deflected all praise or encouragement from people who care most about you?

I did exactly that for a long time. My wife was always present and would *always* give me encouragement after I delivered a speech. Yet, I would always argue against it or explain to her why I sucked. It took me a while to recognize that by this practice I was conditioning myself to believe that my speeches were lousy — that I was lousy.

One experience finally made me realize that I was hurting myself *and* my progression. After a speech in Toastmasters I was approached by two members in the club who were gracious enough to offer me some praise. I did the same thing to them that I'd do to my wife. I brushed it off and started telling them where I messed up, why it was a failure, bla bla

bla. I could almost see it in their eyes, "Man, I'm never complimenting that guy again!"

As I drove home that night with my wife, she echoed what the two members had said, but gracefully added that I had made myself look like an idiot by deflecting their praise with my negativity. I don't know about you, but being called an idiot was enough for me to do some self-analysis. And after examining my actions, I realized that she was right—I was acting like an idiot. That is when I made a commitment not to beat myself up and instead, to search for the good in my speeches, no matter how microscopic. I am not oblivious to where I need to improve, I just don't berate myself for the many mistakes that I make.

This change in attitude has had an incredible effect on me, and if you can relate to this at all, I know it will help you as well. Heed self-encouragement and shun your inner critic. Whether it's "Good job," or "You're great," or "Man, you're awesome," and all those other encouraging one-liners, use them as often as possible to break the dread of imperfection.

The key is to keep on speaking and to keep implementing techniques that work for you. The more opportunities you give yourself to speak the more you will start to build an immunity to the debilitating nervousness and the mental viruses which create it.

It gets easier. Be patient, all the while discovering techniques that will work for you. The extra pressure of "I have to figure this out NOW!" isn't going to help. It will make things worse.

Be humble and marry the idea that it's going to take time. Once I understood that it's something that all speakers go through, I became more patient and willing to endure the pain.

CHAPTER 3

BATHE IN THE FUNDAMENTALS

Let's face it, every single skill has a set of fundamental principles that need to be learned, understood and internalized. Now, that doesn't mean that these fundamental rules were not meant to be broken. I think they should be, at least some of them...*some* of the time.

With this in mind, in order to *productively* break them, you should know what fundamentals you're stomping on. Put another way, one reason to learn the fundamentals is for this very purpose—so that when you break them, you communicate in a manner uniquely yours.

This doesn't mean wagging your finger at all of the essentials, of course. Some of the speaking fundamentals may seem like common sense as you'll find out in this chapter. But there's no perfect template for your speaking persona. We're all different, we all walk, talk, and act differently.

So, in this chapter we'll discuss the basics of public speaking and also *looking* the part. Things such as walking to the stage, gesturing, and even dealing with distractions. There is a lot more depth in this area than you may have thought, but let's pull back the curtain and get our brains wet.

Entering the Arena

In virtually any endeavor there's no substitute for a good start. Clearly that's the case with public speaking. If you can, arrive at least an hour early. And if technology will be part of your presentation, then two to three hours early may be a better idea.

This allows you to become familiar with the stage setup and to make sure all of the audio and visual equipment is working properly. I'm positive Green Day (or the Rolling Stones or whomever) does a sound check before every show and so should you. Something that critical should not be left to chance.

I can't tell you how many times I've been in a situation where there was no audio, no video, no *something*. And I'm not talking about presentations from computer illiterates who thought USB was a college sports team. I've seen people who eat, sleep and breathe computers run into these issues. Fecal matter happens—so be prepared to give your presentation *without* the use of technology, just in case there is a problem. After that tech check, you may actually want to stand there on the stage and view the area where the audience will be seated. Heck, an actual practice run of the speech couldn't hurt either.

Another benefit of arriving early is the opportunity to mingle with the audience members as they arrive. This certainly seems like a cordial thing to do, but it has another important perk. It helps calm nervousness that may arise at the beginning of the presentation.

You have, in fact, cultivated some good will so that there are now friendly faces in the crowd with which to lock eyes, rather than the proverbial "tough crowd." Audience mingling has been conventional wisdom in every book that I've read about public speaking; however, because it sounded so simple, I'd always neglected to do it. Then I attempted the *mingle method* and was amazed at how effective it was — truly it felt like I was talking amongst friends. Chalk one up for conventional wisdom!

From Your Ass to the Stage

Be ready to go as you make your way to the stage. After all, this is the first time the audience will get to see you and, of course, they'll be making snap judgments — they always do. But rather than look at this in a negative vein, consider this an opportunity to sway the crowd before you ever utter a word.

Besides your wardrobe (discussed previously) just how you carry or present yourself enroute to the stage will be under a microscope. Are you slouching with your head down or are you approaching confidently with your shoulders held high? Are you walking slowly (dead man walking?) or do you have a jump to your step? Stand up tall and approach the stage with energy. Power walking or the "quick step" always conveys a confident speaker.

Let's take for example the winner of the 2012 World Championship of Public Speaking, Ryan Avery. When he was introduced to the stage he was running like Forrest Gump. Need more proof? Alright, what about the 2014

World Champion of Public Speaking Dananjaya Hettiarach-chi? He was also jogging to the stage as he was introduced by the Contest Chair. A ploy maybe, but this instantly gives the speaker an aura of confidence before a word is ever spoken. That my friends is what I call getting started off on the best dang foot you got. The fact that champions are doing it validates it even more.

And you should never lose sight of *context* of your speaking engagement. You should have an idea of who is speaking before you, or specifically when you'll be on the agenda so you'll be ready to go when it's your time to speak. Can you imagine the audience's response if you looked startled or surprised at being called to the stage? The term "competent" would probably not surface in their consciousness.

Show Some Teeth

So if the stage is all yours, then what?

Smile.

This will help warm up the audience immediately. You don't want to deal with a tough crowd, and you know what, that goes both ways. Even if you don't feel particularly peachy on the inside, just smile. This is one of those little practices that can have a huge impact on your overall effectiveness. Consider, isn't it much easier to deal with someone who is smiling and friendly as opposed to someone who is poker-faced or even downright hostile? Why would the speaker/audience relationship be any different?

I've noticed that whenever I see a straight-faced new speaker approach the stage, if they're nervous, I can sense it. So be assured, the rest of the audience can sense it too. Oddly enough, this condition creates an uncomfortable tension in the room and only subsides if the speaker gets the audience to laugh or, at least, makes the attempt. On the other hand, if a new speaker gets up with a smile on his or her face—nerves or no—the tension is almost non-existent.

Serving on a team of evaluators, I had the opportunity to help prepare two groups of high school students for a "business plan competition." One of the student groups consisted of six students and the other, four, who had just two weeks' time prior to competition to prepare. The game: to see who could present the best business plan to a group of "investors."

They produced virtual companies, developed dummy web sites, created mock financials—all supporting their "pitch." But while each was a fictitious business opportunity with an imaginary pitch, the preparation they put in was anything but.

Evaluating their presentation skills, it wasn't long before I spotted a glaring issue. Out of the 10 students involved, only one *smiled*. Just one. All were pretty polished with their "lines," but their too sober expressions deadened the impact.

Let's just say that for the majority of my evaluation I beat the (smiling) horse to death. And then, kept beating it for good measure. Expression, countenance—with a smile—it's a game changer!

I later learned that both "teams" placed in the top ten out of a field of 51. Not too shabby.

And I bet they smiled.

Act the Part

Just as you may not feel like smiling when you step on the stage, you may not feel particularly confident either. This, in my experience, is quite understandable. Still, the audience won't detect hesitance if you do a good job of displaying a confident presence.

Smiling is certainly part of this. Good sturdy posture another. And there is another, subtle, but effective tactic. Keep your hands at your sides as you face the audience. For a brand-new speaker this is going to feel awkward. This is a very vulnerable position, almost like the shower curtain falling as you reach for the shampoo.

But with your hands at your side? Now that's a demonstration of confidence!

Need to prove the approach? Test it while talking to strangers (especially in tight proximity) or while merely standing in packed elevator. Keep your hands relaxed at your sides. Your inhibitions will fight you on this one, I promise. When I tested this technique, I found myself doing all kinds of nervous things with my hands and arms such as folding them, touching my ear, my shirt and other fidgety moves.

Among several common "positions" for new speakers is putting their hands together and resting them over their *special places*. This is sometimes referred to as the "fig-leaf position" and it is clearly *not* a demonstration of confidence. Another which reeks of timidity is where the speaker buries his hands in his pockets, then jingles car keys or starts shuffling Pokémon cards (you never know!).

Not only do these show a lack of confidence, but they offer the added danger of distracting the audience. It's hard enough as it is to get listeners to care about what you're saying, but when you add the wagging signs of a third base coach or counting change in your pocket, the audience is forced to make a choice. Do they give their undivided attention to your message or do their minds drift away, escaping by way of your errant behavior?

Rest your hands at your sides as if they were dead weight and remove all the clutter from your pockets. You want to command the stage—so do it.

Talk with Your Hands

Hands at your sides conveys confidence — it is your "starting/resting position." Yet, there will be times to alter that stance, move your hands (and arms), and in doing so, create added impact in your presentation. The most helpful advice regarding such gesturing is to just let them go naturally. Don't think about them or try to force them.

The next time you talk to a friend, pay attention to what you do with your hands. That is what you should strive for. If you put too much mental focus on your gestures, it's going to show. They'll look unnatural, their timing may be disconnected from your words and over-thinking them can knock you off your game.

Though hands at one's sides is both strong and natural, it's not the only confident pose. Another is with arms at the sides, bent at the elbow, where one hand overlaps the other, as they rest between your belly button and sternum. Both of these positions allow you to freely gesture during your speech.

I'd recommend getting comfortable with your hands at your sides first, since it is the most vulnerable (yet confident) position.

After you get that down pat, feel free to experiment. It'll feel weird at first, but with time you'll get used to it. And always, keep the gestures natural and they will add power to your speech.

Go with Who You Know

Similar to gesturing — in that you want their natural flow — the same can be said for your speaking persona. Don't try to be someone else; stick to what you know and be yourself. With new speakers it is natural to want to imitate speakers whom they've observed.

The problem with this is you just make things harder than they have to be. It's one thing to get command of your own insecurities and speaking quirks. Trying to do that while attempting to wear someone else's shoes will eventually be too much for virtually anyone.

Who are you? The audience only has your presence or performance to figure that out. Your gesturing, your manner of speaking (are you conversational or more academic?), your voice (are you trying to sound more like Darth Vader even though you naturally have a higher pitched voice?), the content you choose to speak about (are you qualified and do you even care about your topic?), and lastly, the words you use (do you intentionally use jargon instead of simpler words that mean the same thing?) These will convey who you are as a speaker.

I want you to read through those again...

Can you imagine the amount of mental energy it would take in order to maintain all of these in an alternate persona. I can't tell you in terms of measurement, but it's a plantation sized piece of mental real estate.

By using up all of your energy in a vain effort you're setting yourself up for a bad outing. You only have a finite amount of mental focus available to you and there's an abundance of techniques that go into giving a speech. The more you try to cram into your performance, the easier it is to get lost and have your thoughts completely abandon you.

Having your mind go completely blank in thought during a speech is not fun. As I mentioned earlier, I experienced this firsthand. I knew my material, well-rehearsed and all that good stuff, but my mind shut off before I even hit the one minute mark. I was pacing back and forth for over twenty seconds before my thoughts finally decided to return.

Now, the cause of this was due to nerves and memorization rather than me trying to imitate another speaker's style, but the point I want to make is that it can happen. Why put more pressure on yourself?

The bigger sin associated with imitation is that you lose authenticity. In order to connect with the audience, I believe you need to let yourself shine through. You're unique, so spend time polishing your unique self rather than some other guy.

And look, I'm not saying that you shouldn't do your best to make yourself the best damn *you* possible. In fact, the premise of this book is improvement, for crying out loud. So, if your natural gesturing is too distracting because of over-used gestures, take note of the worn out ones and work to cut them out of your arsenal. Are you a middle-aged rocket scientist trying to talk like a teenage hoodlum or vice versa? Do I even need to address this one?

Are you trying to talk in deeper tones than you are capable of? You can strengthen your voice (which we'll discuss later on) yet ultimately you're stuck with what you've got. It is what it is. Go to work on it, explore it and then make peace with it.

Aren't passionate about a topic? Find something else to talk about. Talking about something you aren't yet well versed in, but that interests you? Hit the books, bub! Do you go out of your way to say "facetious" instead of "kidding"? Unless that's what you'd normally say, stop it.

The secret is to just be you to the extent possible. Not the best Tony Robbins, the best *you*. This takes a giant load of pressure off your shoulders when it comes to delivering your message to an audience. Whoever *you* are at the time of your next presentation, your knowledge, your voice, your whatever, go with *that*.

Be yourself, trust yourself.

Apology Not Accepted

In the arena of public speaking there are several methods you can employ to mask a mistake or lessen its impact on your performance. After all, that's what the great speakers do. By contrast, the last thing you want to do is call attention to any lapse. Whether you've stumbled on a word, lost concentration and in doing so lost your spot, or heck, coughed up a Fruit Loop from breakfast, you can't break stride.

And if there is one thing you should *not do* — it's *apologize*.

It may be tempting, even civil to try to explain yourself, but don't. This is not the NBA Slam Dunk Contest. Those people in chairs in front of you are not *the* judges. Sure, they can definitely judge the effectiveness of your presentation with their subsequent actions — whether or not they take you up on your call to action — but they are present to hear your message, and they do not know exactly what you are "supposed" to say or "how" you are supposed to say it. However imperfect your presentation, you are not required to share those imperfections with them.

Believe it or not, the audience may not have even noticed your slip. I recall a particular speech where the speaker paused for over 10 seconds, at a place that was not particularly powerful. In other words, the audience did not need that much time to reflect on it. Though I recognized it was an unusually long pause, because he kept his eyes on the audience, didn't fidget or begin to pace, and more importantly did not apologize, he was able to continue on, almost as if nothing happened.

My sense of the moment was accurate, as I discovered later. He had indeed lost his place, that sly devil. Yet his response to the situation was impressive and a great example for any speaker to emulate.

Likewise, this "don't apologize" edict goes beyond memory lapse. For example, it also applies to when you jumble or mispronounce a word. Either keep going or if you feel the need, quickly say the word again correctly and move on. In most cases, don't laugh or make light of it, just keep going. If, however, you make a word slip that sounds noticeably odd or silly (even inappropriate) and the audience has noticed, perhaps you could turn that into moment of levity with a snappy one liner. Whatever, make it brief and move on.

It is likewise damning to apologize at the beginning of your speech. An audience should never hear: "Sorry, I am not much of a speaker, so bear with me." Believe me, the audience will have plenty of time to determine the truth of that statement—so don't give them any ammunition.

The secret is to maintain your credibility. And you will keep it as long as you don't (apologetically) give it away.

If You Do Forget...

Since we are human after all, when lapses happen, don't panic. Breathe; but also don't fall back into the "I'm thinking pose." That's when you tilt your head upward and at an angle with your hand on your chin, hoping the Muses will somehow brandish a cue card. Such non-verbal language virtually telegraphs the same impression as if you were to apologize.

Instead, maintain eye contact as if everything is going according to plan. Then you have a few options to buy your memory some time to refocus.

The main defense would be to speak off the cuff momentarily about something related to your subject, that is until you get back on track which shouldn't be a problem if you know your material well as discussed earlier.

Another thing you can do is repeat the last word or phrase that you said, particularly if it was something important. Particularly if it was something important. Something important. Important. You get the idea. Keep in mind that this can come off as awkward if you repeat the last word or phrase of every single sentence, so be sure to do the unthinkable and *prepare* as much as possible.

You can also talk slower or pause once you realize that you're lost, but try to not to pause mid-sentence or it may seem awkward and draw more attention to it. That's like if I were to...

These tips are designed to give you as much time as possible to regain your train of thought.

Stage Movement

Some truths regarding public speaking: the podium is stationary, but the speaker is not. The words are static, but their potential is dramatic. Is there a way to reconcile these realities?

When a speaker is nervous there is a natural tendency to pace back and forth—actually walking from one side of the stage to the other—and back. When I gave my first speech, I'd have won the Wandering World Championship if there were such a thing.

I talked while moving from one spot to another, stopping just enough to rotate my body in the opposite direction, and then making my way back to the other side of the bridge. No variation, just left to right, right to left, in the same predictable, path. You could call that distracting. But *ridiculously* distracting might be more accurate—so promise never to follow in my footsteps.

So, I was advised at the time to plant my feet and to only *move with purpose*. It was a great piece of advice, but I clearly misunderstood the part about "with a purpose." Today I can clarify. Purposeful movement is intentional movement, and can be divided into at least three main categories. Before we go through them, I must clarify, this section is about any movement from one spot on the stage to another. Gesturing and other in place movements are crucial in order to paint the audience a picture. But, these fall under the category of gesturing because they don't require that you move from one position on the stage to another.

Now, let's begin.

One category could be purposeful or forceful movement as a way to emphasize a key point. These can be just about anything. Taking forceful steps toward the audience to demonstrate a powerful point is a simple example (this could be accompanied by a powerful gesture with a clenched fist to match your movement). If it makes sense to what is being said and how it is being said, chances are it has a purpose. This is good.

Another can be described as "in-story" movement. For example, the actual movements being described. Say your story takes place while jogging around your neighborhood, why not jog a few steps in dramatic fashion? Maybe the story takes place on the dance floor, why not show the audience those funky dance moves? And unless you're Michael Jackson's protégé, avoid the full concert, please.

The other part of this "in-story" movement can be during a character to character interaction, or during dialogue, there is the option to take a step from your present position in order to differentiate between characters. Another way to explain it would be to pivot your body 90 degrees to signify a different character's perspective, and then pivot back and forth as necessary (use sparingly as it can be overdone).

The last is your stage positioning as a tactical part of your presentation. Examples include where to start on the stage, where to move for each point in the body, and where to go for the conclusion. These should be thought out in advance. If the speech has a moving through time (then to now) feel, it may be a good idea to have a spot for each point in time, a logical one at that. Here is an example: Begin the speech in the center of the stage, then move to the right side of the stage (audience's left) for the first point, back to center stage for the next point, and then to the left (audience's right). Move back to the center for the conclusion. This is a basic, yet effective way to do it.

Another variation of this is to separate your main points into different parts of the stage. Again, the middle, to the right side, and then the left is an effective way to do this. This helps the audience separate the points in their own minds which could help them remember your message.

Those are examples of what to do, but what's wrong with random movement? The simple answer is that it's distracting. If the audience catches on to predictable pacing from a speaker, they'll start to watch only for that. The speaker's words and information will no longer matter. That's not good. It also signals to the audience that the speaker may be nervous, as opposed to confident.

Remember, there is no problem with moving on stage, just make it purposeful.

Connect with Eye Contact

There's no contact like eye contact. Your words and your message will have greatest impact when each audience member feels like you are talking to them personally — one on one. Yet, there is more to it, as I have observed while on the receiving end of a speech as part of an audience.

As that eye contact is made (sometimes repeatedly made) the listener becomes more connected with the speaker — *be it intellectually or personally*—as if they feel obligated to continue paying attention, even after the initial eye contact has been broken.

Perhaps it's an example of the psychological principle of reciprocity—where someone gives us something and we feel obligated to return the favor. In this case the speaker gives by *elevating*, even flattering audience members by speaking *to them* and they, in turn, reciprocate by giving their undivided attention.

Okay, so how do we hone this power over the audience?

For one, remember, the goal is to make eye contact with everyone in the room. Depending on the size of the audience, this is either possible or it isn't. In the case of it being impossible (too many attendees) try to cover all sections of the room, so that it gives the illusion of giving attention to everyone in the audience. To keep the whole group engaged, then, avoid looking only at a single person or section for the duration of your remarks.

Hold that eye contact for as long as it takes to complete a thought. Don't arbitrarily shower your audience with a random visual spray, but let it fall on a single spot for a single thought—then move on naturally to another member of the audience.

It's not about merely scanning the room with a soft glance, it's about truly making a connection and making it difficult for the audience to avoid that connection. With something as intimate as eye contact, if you've done it properly, the audience will have a hard time ignoring your invitation to connect.

Turn It Up

Can you be heard all the way to the back of the room? You understand—that is your mission. If the audience can't hear you, you will have failed, no matter how good your content may be.

No, not talking about shouting. I mean talking loud enough and with authority. Even in situations where a microphone is present, you'll still have to use your voice with purpose. If you want to emphasize a point such as in character yelling or shouting, then you'll actually need to shout, even with a microphone.

It's a skill you see many singers use, pulling back from the mic as they raise their voices and it is something that requires practice. When I first started giving speeches at Toastmasters I felt that I spoke too softly, at a level more like every day chit-chat. Early evaluations confirmed this. I needed to speak up and I needed to improve the quality of my voice. (Later in the book I will provide some practice tips for how to do this.)

Furthermore, what if you have to compete against audible distractions while on stage? You might need to speak even louder. The Toastmasters club that I attend used to meet in a room that had a freezer in the back that would always turn on at random times during the meeting. We actually debated whether to have the building maintenance department take it out or unplug it, but in the end, we decided to keep it to help prepare the speakers for distractions in the real world.

You never know.

Diversify Your Vocal Portfolio

The audience should be able to hear you throughout your entire speech. However, you can't be monotone. Vocal variety is a hot topic when it comes to speaking. It demands you have to vary your voice—higher pitched, lower pitched, adding warmth (sincerity), etc. You want to be interesting. You want the characters in your stories to be interesting. Vocal variety is the key. There's really no special trick to varying your voice, just that you need to vary it. Match it to the emotion that you're trying to convey to the audience. That's it.

Despite the use of varying tones, you still need to be loud enough with all of them. At one point, I incorporated whispering into a part of one of my speeches in Toastmasters, but had a problem when those in the back of the room couldn't hear me. For that specific case, I was given the advice not to actually whisper, but to imply whispering. To do that it was necessary to change my tone to a softer level of talking, but loud enough to be heard.

I have a blast practicing for vocal variety. I learned that I have many more voices and volume levels at my disposal than I ever thought. Think of your voice as an instrument that, with practice, can improve your performances. Play it well.

The Speed of Words

Another item that gets lumped in with vocal variety, is the pace at which we speak. Are you a fast talker or a slooow talker? Doesn't matter. Chances are you'll likely pick up the pace while in front of a crowd, so you better plan for this reality.

As an aspect of vocal variety, it's something that could and should vary. There will be places in your speech where you can speed up, and other times you'll slow down. Shifting gears is a means to keep the audience interested.

Even with preparation, we have a tendency to talk faster when we are in front of a crowd. Driven by even a micron of anxiety, it almost appears as if we want the pain to end, so we rush through our content as fast as possible. Unfortunately, this does not go unnoticed. I recall a couple of my own speeches where it seemed that I was just talking at the audience, rather than to them. With that type of relationship, it will be hard get the audience to retain or even care about the message being shared with them.

I'm naturally a fast talker, so my earliest speeches were like a drag race. Decline of numbers — go! In what was planned as a six-minute and forty-five second speech, I finished in five. I was definitely in a sprint mode to the finish line.

The better way, regardless of your normal speaking pace, is to go slower. The reason is control. You'll appear more controlled in your delivery and thus more credible to the audience. Keep in mind that I said slow-er. This doesn't mean that you pay tribute to Ben Stein — that man talks slow. Find a happy medium. And if you want to rap, stringing together words quickly during portions of your speech, that's fine too. But you dictate.

Give the audience a roller coaster ride of vocal output and maybe, just maybe, they'll stay with you until the end.

Watch the Clock

I want to add a small bit about the timing of your speech. Usually speakers are given (think mandated) a time slot in which to fill. Don't go over that slice of time.

I mention this in conjunction with the importance of understanding our natural tendency to "speed up" during the actual speech. Granted, it's more acceptable in my eyes to end sooner rather than going over the allotted time; however, ending too soon or going over the time allotment creates problems for somebody else: the next speaker, the master of ceremonies, the audience, etc.

Finishing in a timely manner shows both professionalism and courtesy — two nice qualities to display.

Deal with It

Distractions during your speech can come in a variety of forms. Attendees may be coming in late through the doors, they may exit early, they may break for the restroom, phones may go off, freezer motors may kick on, or outside construction work may rattle the building. The list doesn't end there, but your response to them is what's important.

If it is something the audience absolutely can't ignore, you should pause and wait for the noise to fade before continuing. It's not necessary to address it or call out the disruption or the disruptor directly, yet it may be worth mentioning perhaps by making a quick joke to ease any tension created.

Humor is an excellent tool for escaping just about any situation. Something as simple as "Moving on" or (if you trust your game) "Turn off your damn phones, people!" However, if it's an individual creating the ruckus, go easy on them. You're not looking to reprimand anyone; just keep things light and easy until you can continue.

If it's something abrupt that doesn't seem to capture the audience's attention, just continue talking through it as if it never happened—the perpetrator also saves face.

It's even possible there may be hecklers, too. My recommendation would be to avoid showing any anger or resentment. If an audience member disagrees with something you said, let them know you'd be happy to hear them out after you finish up. (I can hear you thinking, "But what if they try to assault me?" Sorry, you're on your own.)

Seriously though, your objective, no matter what the distraction may be, is to maintain control while you have the stage. Keep the speech moving forward.

I've done my best to cover everything regarding fundamentals in this chapter. There are a lot of things to think about, believe me, I know. However, with practice they'll become second nature.

Later on we'll discuss means of practicing but here's a quick tip: Don't think about all that there is to know. When you get started on your journey, focus on only one or two pieces to work on at a time and understand that it's going to take time. Throw out the need to be perfect! If you can maintain a beginner's mindset, one of curiousness and excitement toward speaking, you'll find learning to be more pleasant.

CHAPTER 4

THE BLOOD AND GUTS: SPEECH CONTENT

As much fun as it would be to get up there and ramble on about whatever you'd like, there needs to be a bit of structure and some reason for the audience to listen.

Do you have information to share? Are you there to entertain? Are you looking to persuade the audience to your point of view? Do you want to inspire? Debate? Sell your cookbooks? Those are some of the most common purposes of a speech and all of which are fine reasons to prepare and deliver a message to an audience.

To be clear, this chapter isn't about the different purposes of a speech, but it's going to touch on the fundamentals that could benefit any speech including general tips for constructing a speech and even remembering your main points.

Before we begin, there's something you should do *before* constructing your next presentation. Know what it is you want the audience to do after your speech. Be crystal clear about it, because if you aren't, how can you expect the audience to be? This can serve as the North Star as you prepare your message—the focus around which your speech should be built.

And as always, you're unique to this process. These are proven *guidelines* to make your speech edible; however, they aren't all encompassing. Human creativity knows no bounds and if you can think of a novel way to capture the attention of your audience or implant your message into their consciousness, I say go for it...or at least try it out.

Let's begin.

Sculpting Your Speech

An important piece of information before constructing your speech is to know who your audience is going to be. You wouldn't want to talk about how to skin an animal to a group of PETA members—the message isn't going to hit its mark (at least where you want it to hit). Instead, a better message would be how you plan to save the furry, scaly, feathery critters.

And more importantly, you'll want to talk about something you're qualified to address and something about which you're legitimately passionate. It's hard to fake passion. In other words, stay with a subject you know. If not, the audience will know.

Once you've selected the topic, think through the main or significant points of your speech before getting them down on paper. If you do write down ideas, just jot down a few words about each. Having logged them, it's then you can really put thought to them. Even mentally organize them, and consider in what order you'd like to deliver them.

Once you get the main ideas ingrained into your head, write a simple outline on paper (intro, body, and conclusion) to build your presentation's skeletal structure. Over-think and over-research your topic. Even though you may not use all the information you gather, the process will still help you clarify your thoughts. And with a potential bonus. Should you lose your spot in the speech delivery, having this info may allow you to talk about something related until you can get back on track.

Write as you would talk. I used to first write out my entire speech and then refine it over time. It never felt right, though. It didn't feel natural. The best way to explain it is that when I wrote the thoughts down on paper before intimately thinking them through, I'd rely on the words written on the paper rather than where they originally came from—my brain.

It was like a crutch, I no longer looked inside my head for the content, but instead I'd try and think of the words that I wrote down. It's like an unnecessary middle-man. For example, instead of thinking of the actual topic (mental pictures and passionate reasons why I care about it) I would think only of the words I wrote down. Seriously, the words. Like the ones you're reading now. I would think of an image of my computer screen, the digital document, and then the words and the order that I wrote them in.

I would essentially be remembering a script and thus be dependent on it. I also feel that it contributed to the mental blackout that I experienced during one of my speeches. I can't be too sure about this though, I'd have to discuss it with Fear to see how much of a factor he was, and he's not much help.

Another thing is that it made me unforgiving toward myself because I didn't give myself any slack with how I could deliver my words to the audience. But, as soon as I made the changes, I was no longer "forced" to recite my speech as it was written.

So now, after I organize my thoughts, I put them into an outline—a very simple outline. However, instead of writing out word for word what I want to discuss, I'll only write down the main points that I want to talk about, and in as few words as possible. That way, I am not forced to have to use a single set of words to lead up to and even describe my main points. I still have an end goal in mind—the point I want to describe to the audience—but now I am free to lead up to it as I please, whichever words flow into my mind. This really brought down a layer of stress associated with speaking, because now there was a lot less I had to worry about and remember. And of course, less opportunity for my *internal judge* to criticize me.

Let me explain about the internal judge. For example, if you write out your speech word for word, and then memorize it word for word, you've now been chained to those words. Basically, you've set a goal for yourself come speech day. But, if you stumble on your words, or leave something out because you forget, there is a sense of failure. And we like to judge ourselves and bludgeon ourselves into submission for such failures.

Well, let me tell you something about my judge: he was a raging maniac on steroids. He could turn a mispronounced "the" into Armageddon. No joke. And a judge heaving out criticism is hardly favorable for anyone who wants to improve at something, especially something that requires a "walk the plank" mentality each time you do it.

So my point is why not tap directly into the fountain of knowledge—your thoughts—as opposed to writing them on paper and then trying to cram them back into your memory from the paper?

Do You Remember Now?

As far as remembering goes, there are memory tricks available. I know this was still lingering in the back of your mind Mr. or Mrs. Perfectionist, but worry not, for the Method of Loci, more commonly known as the Memory Palace, was constructed just for you to remember your speech points.

It's the same fundamental technique used by participants in the World Memory Championships in order to remember all sorts of things such as card decks, two-digit numbers, alphabet, number sequences, etc.

There is a great TED Talk by Joshua Foer that describes the history about memorization techniques and how you can implement them. It's available on the Internet and is well worth your time. In case you're unfamiliar with TED — well, here's how they put it on their website — *TED is a nonprofit devoted to spreading ideas, usually in the form of short, powerful talks (18 minutes or less).*

Foer describes that we remember things easier when associated with spatial awareness. Let's take your house as an example. With this structure you are able to create a story.

Perhaps at your front door there is a waiter holding a menu. This could be used to remember your opening about a dining experience gone wrong at a restaurant.

Then in your living room sits an elephant wearing Mickey Mouse ears, a hint to remind you of an experience at Disneyland.

Picture a room that you are familiar with. Now picture in the middle of the room a huge red phone with neon green buttons. Maybe there was an important call that changed your life — there's your cue.

And continue on and on through as many rooms as you need to add memory clues.

Here is a basic summary:

- Think of a building that you are familiar with. You want to be able to easily recall rooms, storage places, bathrooms, etc. The more familiar you are with the selected building, the better.
- Decide on a logical route through your building. Your movement throughout it should progress logically. You

don't want to have to double-up on the same room with two separate memory triggers or it could get confusing.

- Place cues in each room that is included in your route. These are imagined pictures in your mind to help you recall your speech points. The wilder and crazier the images, the easier they are to remember. For example, if you needed to remember a story about a fishing trip, picture a giant fish sitting on the toilet in one of your rooms. It can be anything as long as it helps jog your memory.

- Draw out a basic floor plan of your building to get an even greater familiarity with your chosen location.

- Now go on a journey in your mind. Start out at your first room, go to the next, then the next, and the next until you complete your speech. Each room should have some oddity or image associated with it that ties it to what you want to remember for your speech. The amount of points you want to remember is up to you. I would recommend keeping it to a minimum although you're only limited by your imagination and your ability to remember it all.

Give it a test run in your mind. It could be for anything that you want to remember and is not limited to remembering speeches. You'll never have to write your grocery list down on paper again! But, there is a downside. If you forget, don't expect any leeway from your significant other because, "I forgot the list" ain't gonna fly.

Start Fast

Even interested audiences get bored quickly. Disinterested groups may need even more "encouragement." TV and film producers know it, advertisers surely know it and you should too! It's absolutely critical to get the audience's attention as rapidly as possible.

I don't know the exact number for how much time you have before the audience tunes you out, but it's not much. Ten, 20, 30 seconds? It's definitely not *minutes*. So what can you do to start things off with a bang? There's a pretty small list of effective ways for getting the audience's attention, here they are:

- Story or vignette
- Powerful question that involves the audience actually responding (by voice or raising of hand)
- A powerful rhetorical question meant to get the audience to think and consider
- Quotations
- Humor, often ironic
- Shocking (counter-intuitive) statement or statistic

Before getting into the specifics of each of these, I want to clarify that this literally means *as soon as you start shooting words out of your mouth*. Definitely not after you give some lame, strained or mundane "Hi, I'm Johnny and I'm some random person here to talk to you about some random subject." You should have been introduced beforehand, but if not, think of something better to say than that. Keep in mind, this is *about them*. Not you.

On the other hand, I have no objections to a sincere greeting—*after you've secured their attention*. Even something as simple as "Good evening, ladies and gentlemen." I would encourage you to customize this to your specific crowd as well. For example, if you're speaking to students that currently attend your alma mater (the school that reluctantly graduated you) the greeting might be: "Good evening, fellow whatchamacallits," or whatever it is they call themselves in that group or organization. Then go...

Tell Me a Story, Daddy

Let's face it, we all love stories. Ever since we were children we'd love hearing a captivating story. Something in us perks up when someone starts telling one—we relate, we remember, we react. We're trained like Pavlov's salivating dogs when they heard the bell and thought it was time to eat. So naturally, a story is a good way to engage the audience so that they'll continue to listen.

There are different ways you can implement a story. You can tell them straight up that you're going to tell them a story—which is good because they'll be tuned in right away. You can start the story neck deep in drama or action—yet recognize it might take a while for the audience to understand what's going on, which may cause confusion.

On the other hand, it could also be a good thing because they'll be focused on trying to figure it out. It's a good idea to experiment with both to see what's more effective. You can also begin by telling the very last part of your story, and later on in your speech, bring the audience back in time with you.

You can't go wrong with a story.

Let Me Ask You Something

Questions signal to the brain that it's time to think. And that's what you want the audience to do, think *about your question*, that is. In order to do that, you better have a darn good question, one that is pertinent to what you will be talking about. And the answer should not be *predictable*. This goes for both audience involvement questions—that require their response—and also rhetorical questions.

This is more an aspect of *delivery* that probably belongs in the previous chapter, but since it is related to questions specifically, I'll cover it here. When you ask a question, it's extremely important that you pause before you continue. The audience needs sufficient time to think about what you're asking them.

Put yourself in that position, where someone is asking you a question and as soon as you start to think about it, they pin you with another question or worse, start talking about something else. Annoying, yeah?

This was a very bad habit of mine during my speeches. Even after I was alerted to it, it still continued to be a problem even when I thought I was pausing sufficiently, but nope. So I offer this because it shows that our perception of time can be distorted while we're up in front of an audience.

So ask powerful questions, get the audience to think, and *give them the time* to do so.

What Somebody Else Said

There are people all over the world that say awesome things. Why not plagiarize them, er quote them, that is? And you might want to throw in the name of the individual you're quoting to avoid actual plagiarism. Just a thought.

Using quotations is an excellent way to get the audience to reflect. Again, relevance is key, making sure the quotation is relevant to your speech. You wouldn't want to throw in a random quote just because it sounded cool and intelligent. Sure, the person you're quoting might have sounded cool and intelligent, but you won't if it doesn't tie into your speech.

When searching for a quote to fit into your speech, avoid quotes that everyone and their mom and her dayshift supervisor has heard before. "I have a dream..." - Martin Luther King, or John F. Kennedy's "Ask not what your country can do for you..." Excellent quotes, excellent speeches, but they've been beaten into oblivion.

Ideally, you'll want to use quotes from famous people because it builds credibility with the audience. However, there are ways around this that could make your speech a hit. What if you quoted an infant, or your pet? As I write this, I'm imagining a sixty-something-year-old barking or babbling in baby-talk. "Babies always give the best advice. Just the other day I asked my baby granddaughter for some advice, and you know what she said? "Boo da ba DA!" Incredible. Who knows what it meant, but I needed to hear it." Funny, right? Good times, brain, good times. Refocus.

So here's another available option for starting a speech in an interesting way — with a quote.

Add a Little Humor to Your Life

Oh, Humor, how you make us laugh.

This approach is a personal favorite of mine. Making people laugh is an exquisite way to warm the audience so that they'll become receptive to your message.

But does this mean that you get up there and right away tell them a "your momma" joke? Fat chance. You want your humor to be related to your message or at least relevant to the audience or the event at which you are speaking. Self-deprecating humor — making yourself the butt of the joke — is a very safe form of humor. After all, you don't want to alienate anyone from the crowd by making them the butt of the joke (even if they deserve it).

"Jokes" in general, however, are not a good choice because their impact is so unpredictable within any group of individuals. Unless the sole purpose of the speech is to offend or disconcert, avoid telling them because that is precisely what can happen. And if the joke *bombs* and you're left in complete silence, you'll have to dig yourself out of an even tougher situation.

Adding humor to stories (in dialogue especially) should be a staple. Let the characters in your stories come up with *the funny*. You can change your voice, your body language or facial expressions to make them come alive. And the characters can pretty much say anything, after all, you didn't say it.

We all can relate to exaggeration a bit from time to time. Well, a way to be funny is to *over-exaggerate*. For example, like when you told your friends that you've been going on *a lot* of dates lately. But the truth is, lunch with your mom is the only date you've been on in years. I know, I know, I'm sorry — that's full of exaggeration on my part.

Another simple way to get some laughs is to talk about something that happened at the event before your turn to speak — this is a *callback* in comedy lingo. Whether the host or the speaker before you said something funny, call it back and make a reference to something related to what they said or what was funny about it. But, do it in your own way and not so that it attempts to make fun of the person who initially said it.

Another thing you can use is an amusing or interesting experience you've had recently. Maybe while in the city of the event, while you were getting ready, or something virtually in real time. The sheer immediacy of the item can be enough to make it relevant to your saying it. And, if you can somehow weave it into your speech's purpose, do it.

Recognize the use of humor in your speech first alleviates some tension — for both the speaker and for the audience. But it may also have the added benefit of setting apart your presentation from others on the docket.

I had an experience that gave me some insight into this humor thing. The event was the Toastmasters International Speech Contest in which I was a contestant. Well, as luck (or bad luck depending on how you look at it) would have it, I was uniquely positioned where I was able to hear all of the other competitors before my time at the podium. We (the competitors) were allowed to speak about anything, just as long as it was "inspirational" and clean enough for grandma. So, each of those competent speakers (myself included) took on the theme of "inspirational" and battled it out in three divisions, where a finalist from each was determined.

Each of those presentations I witnessed was not merely polished, but also dignified (if not subdued) and must have put the judges to the test. As near as I could tell, there was only one glaring difference between the other speeches and mine, which was confirmed by the audience. During *my* speech there were several outbreaks of the infectious disease known as *laughter* — the belly variety.

No, it was not totally expected. But yes, I added into that speech, places for targeted audience response. Going in, I didn't know how the other speakers would handle the topic. Yet, as matter of fact, it was humor that made the difference on that occasion. And in the judges' eyes, it was enough to win the day!

To give you a little context, the message of my contest speech was to treat people with respect, and especially if you wanted their help! I learned this the hard way in an experience I had with my bank at the *wise* age of 16. Let's just say that it involved my account being overdrawn. Maybe you can relate.

Frankly, I completely mishandled my attempt at gaining sympathy from the service rep. Instead of easing in with kindness in hopes of getting my money back, I reared back and gave her hell. As you can imagine, it didn't work out as

I had hoped. Anyway, here's an example of humor from my speech that I used to ease the audience into my bank story.

"The experience that I had was with my bank. Now, I'm not gonna tell you the name of the bank, but it rhymes with "Ells Argo."

The audience followed up with this:

"HAHAHAHAHAHAHAHA."

Get it? I told them I *wasn't* going to tell them the name of the bank, and then I pretty much did! Funny? Okay, maybe you had to have been there. They laughed. I promise.

Now look, my mom says I've got a little wit, but I'm not a comedian by any stretch. As you see from my example, humor does not have to be complex. It can be simple and subtle or even slapstick. At any rate, my experience makes a strong case for adding *funny* when you can.

In case you're not naturally funny, don't worry. It can be learned. It doesn't mean you'll be the next Lt. Frank Drebin from the movie *The Naked Gun*, but then again, I'm not sure anyone could fill those shoes.

Those in sales also understand the power of humor and it's because they know very well that a cold prospect has their "you ain't sellin' me" defenses up, and in order to lower them, they use humor. You should, too.

Shock 'Em Dead

"I set my 7-year-old daughter on fire." Pause. Pretty shocking, eh?

Your shocking statement or statistic should be something that elicits emotion from the audience. The statement needs to be relevant to your topic. In the example above, maybe it's a story about how a father gave his daughter a book that set her curiosity ablaze. Or maybe he did so literally, with kerosene, and the point of the speech fire safety. No? Too harsh? You think you could do better? Everybody's a critic I tell ya!

An interesting fact or statistic is another variation—particularly one that is not well known. For instance, "Humans will be asleep for twenty-five years over a lifetime (assuming an average life expectancy of seventy-five years and eight hours of sleep a day). Life's not all that long after all it seems."

A corollary to this is when obligated to use otherwise boring facts or statistics, you'd want to turn the data into something the audience can imagine or get their heads around. For example, every time I hear someone recite the speed of light, my brain shuts down. I have absolutely nothing to relate to "one hundred eighty-six thousand two hundred and eighty-two miles per second."

But, if you included a point or points of reference, that could change everything. Say, "If you were to move at the speed of light, you'd be able to run around the earth seven and a half times per second." Now that's something I could sink my brain into—or sink into my brain? Either way. It's much better than giving a dry factoid.

There are countless ways to use this technique. Just keep it relevant and make sure it gets the audience's attention.

Structurally Sound

Your speech should have a structure that is easy to follow. Don't count on your message being well received and acted upon if the audience is confused. A popular axiom in the speaking world is: "Tell them what you're gonna tell them, tell them, and then tell them what you've told them."

I love it because it's so simple. The axiom explained: In your introduction, give the audience a hint as to what they'll learn from your speech, then in your body give them the details, and in your conclusion give a brief recap of what they learned. The trick is taking this simple format — it's less about glamour and excitement and more about helping the audience retain what they've heard — and delivering it in an exciting and interesting way in order to keep the audience engaged.

I will add though, that even if you stuck to this format in its purest, most basic form, there are worse things in life. In other words, if you actually tell the audience the points you are going to cover ("we'll be covering this, that, and the other thing") then go over them one by one, and finally, give a brief summary listing out what you've talked about, you wouldn't go wrong. Just don't forget to tie it all together with a single call to action, which we'll discuss later.

Transition Through the Journey

Also on the topic of structure and speech navigation, let's talk about transitions. These help the audience follow from one point to the next. These can be very blatant such as first point, second point, third point, next, then, finally, and other chronological or logical transitions. But these aren't the end all.

Stories are a great way to keep your audience right along with you. Since they are naturally told in a logical manner, it's not necessary to make extra emphasis on the transition words. The story should organically move in and out of the different scenes. Using a phrase like "Let's go back five years," is an example of a transition you could use to prepare the audience for your story.

Another possible use for transitions is what Craig Valentine—the 1999 World Champion of Public Speaking—calls *transition teases*. These are used to heighten the interest of your audience so that they'll want to hear more. For this to work, you'll need to have something that they really want or don't want.

On Valentine's website he offers 52 free speaking tips and in one of them he explains that there are two approaches to the transition teases:

- Silver Spoon Approach: This involves telling the audience the benefits they'll get if they follow your next point. So the benefit should be something that they want.

  Example: If you listen to this next point, you will learn the secret of all secrets that took me 2000 years and trillions of dollars to uncover...

- Verbal Knife Approach: This is based on finding the pain your audience is having, and twisting the knife. You want to describe the pain, get them to express their pain, and then offer them a cure. This approach helps them get away from what they don't want.

  Example: Raise your hand if you're a perfectionist? Okay, now raise your hand if being a perfectionist creates a barrier that blocks you off from trying new things due to the fear of failing or making mistakes? Well, if you listen to this next point, you'll discover how to overcome this barrier and build immunity to the fear of failing...

Don't get too hung up on which specific transition words you should use. There are endless ways to do it. Remember, the reason why you add the transitions is to prepare the audience for your next point, and with Valentine's advice, even to create curiosity and build anticipation so that they'll want to listen.

Tie Your Main Points to Something

You've told them where you are going to take them, now take them. Each of the points you make should be tied to an example. If you feel it is important enough to prepare a speech and deliver it then it should be important enough to make your information last in the minds of your audience. Remember, they don't have the luxury of watching the replay or the highlights of your speech on the nightly news. A few people may take notes, but this is the exception rather than anything remotely typical. So, you must give them a mental souvenir by tying your points to something more remarkable than mere facts.

I used to think it was good enough just to have my points articulated. After all, my words were so amazingly profound (or at least they were in my mind). That can be a problem though. We know what we mean, but not everyone views things from the same vantage point. So to help steer the audience to our vantage point, we must tie our main ideas to something that everyone can grasp.

Here are some examples:

Story

Stories. Stories. Stories. There is a reason you keep reading about stories. They're excellent vehicles for delivering information and they're easy for the audience to remember. I had the honor of attending a live speech by distinguished motivational speaker Les Brown and he declared, "Never make a point without telling a story and never tell a story without making a point." Well said, Mr. Brown.

Try to think of stories from your life, and lessons that you learned. Share those lessons by polishing those stories. You absolutely cannot go wrong with a story.

Acronym

An acronym is another useful way to tie your message to the audience's memory card. Everyone's got an acronym these days and, for the most part, it's because they work. We have one in our Toastmasters club, which is R.I.O.T. It's an abbreviation for Relax, It's Only Toastmasters. And therein lies the trick. Keep them short and as something that the audience members can clearly picture in their minds.

If your acronym was Z.E.R.F.I.X.L.M. — zer...fix...elm? — it's not going to be remembered. Plain and simple. You want them short and sweet. And better still, the word should be fun and evoke a familiar image.

Metaphor/Analogy/Simile

Metaphors, analogies and similes can help take a complex idea and break it down into something more easily understood. In other words, these tools help make connections in our minds by using comparisons. We hear these all the time.

Similes use the words "like" or "as" to compare two different things: "The job interview was like a nightmare." These are pretty straight forward.

Metaphors compare elements by identifying them or implying they are something else. For example, "Fear is a wall that prevents us from fulfilling our dreams."

Have you been in any "heated" arguments lately? Bam. Metaphor. Did that girl or guy of your dreams, "shoot you down?" I can do this all day. Metaphors are more direct than similes. They don't beat around the bush. They tell you that something is something else, not merely *like* it.

Analogies are similar to both metaphors and similes in that they compare things. But, these are a bit more thorough. From the Merriam-Webster online dictionary:

"Analogy: A comparison of two things based on their being alike in some way."

The analogy is more detail-oriented. It picks out a similar characteristic shared by two things and then compares them. Here is an example: Motivation is to action as wood is to fire.

They're all useful and can be twisted in all sorts of directions. Keep them simple and fun. And remember, you want the idea *scorched* into your audience's mind. Hehehe (cynical laughter).

Audience Involvement

There is yet another option — audience involvement. This is different than merely asking a question and having them participate by the show of hands. For getting a point across, you can create an actual activity. You're looking for something that is able to *drill home your point* and get the audience involved in the process. It should also be fun.

Here is a quick example of an activity to involve the audience. Say your speech is on how to properly give instructions or guidance. You might give each member of the audience a sheet of paper and tell them to make an airplane. But not just any airplane, it has to be the same one as an example you've shown them (pre-folded so they can't see how you did it). When they fail to build it in like manner, you can point to how not providing them with the necessary instructions to complete a task was not a good idea. At least not if you want the job done correctly.

You've just read about four powerful ways to tie your main points to something concrete so that the audience will both understand your ideas, and remember them long enough (even on the drive home?) to benefit from them. Asking too much? Probably. At least you'll remember that you tried. Be as creative as you'd like, just don't lose sight of why you are marrying your point to whichever method you decide upon.

Choose Your Words Carefully

And now we move into the actual words, themselves. With some guidelines. A reminder I like to use: If our brain can complete a pattern, it will.

This means that if we can anticipate the next words out of someone's mouth, we will. Either out loud or surely in our heads. Occasionally during a conversation, I'll find myself consciously trying to complete the thought of what someone else is saying, before they say it. I admit, not the best conversational skill, but it illustrates an important point.

You can see the problem—in advance. If a speaker is predictable, the audience is no longer hanging on his or her every word. We want the audience to listen to us. As humans we enjoy new information and ideas that we haven't heard before. If you can avoid being predictable, you'll keep the audience interested in what you're saying—this applies throughout your entire speech.

What makes speech predictable? It's those clichés, common axioms, overused quotations, and all the mundane subjects and tired references that dull your audience's attention. Try to mix it up when describing your main points. Think of creative new ways to tell them.

I always give an imaginary thumbs up to a writer or speaker whenever I read or hear a new way of saying something that typically gets communicated with a cliché. For example, instead of saying "I was scared to death," you could describe it in more detail, "I was scared. My heart was pounding like a sledgehammer against a piece of aluminum sheet metal and my thoughts dried up like a puddle on a scalding mid-summer afternoon. I knew I was dead."

It ain't easy. It takes some brain effort because we're so accustomed to speaking in platitudes—so we don't have to think. But, if you want to keep the audience's attention, it's worth it to try. I'm guilty of this, but *I'm giving it the old college try*.

And then there are words that simply have *más* power. More emotion. More betterness. If there ever were an element to try and make perfect, or as close to it as possible, your words are it. If you watch the news, you'll notice that they use powerful words which convey a strong feeling—either negative or positive. You can usually discern instantly which way the particular news outlet wants you to feel about it, too. Interesting for a "news" outlet that should be reporting facts from a neutral perspective. Whoops, got sidetracked a bit. But they demonstrate the point.

When a media outlet has a story about a "conspiracy theorist," what image comes to your mind? It might conjure up images of a crazy person living in their mother's basement and reviewing news clippings about the JFK assassination.

What I've noticed is that it works quite effectively at disparaging someone—whether it's accurate or not. What about a "kook?" Same thing. It gives me a strong picture of what is trying to be conveyed. Words are freaking powerful I tell ya.

Think about euphemisms as well. This is the opposite of using strong, concrete words. It's about transforming them into a more mild or pleasant word. Have you ever been "let go" from a job? You have? No, you haven't. You got *fired*. And what's this I hear about your child being "difficult"? No, no, no, he's just a little jerk. So you can either euphemize—kinda like euthanize, but for words—or pick words that are on steroids. The choice is yours. I don't mean be offensive just to get some shock value although with a clever opening you might be able to get away with it. What I do mean is using words that have emotion and that create an image in the listener's mind.

Other things to consider are clarity and simplicity. Avoid jargon and overly technical terms, unless your crowd is well-versed in the subject. Sometimes the simplest word is the best word. If the audience needs to take an unnecessary amount of time to understand what you just said, they may miss your follow-up thoughts and end up getting lost or confused. That is, if they keep listening.

Try and use action words that have heart and soul. "The dog zoomed across the yard and slammed into the wall" sounds better than "The dog went across the yard and bumped into the wall." Words that denote action such as ran, darted, zipped, flipped, kicked, and jumped. Those words *deliver!* They create a picture and they do it instantly.

Don't be wordy. Get straight to the point. Don't say "In view of the fact that we as Homo sapiens tend to act as emotional creatures...", instead say, "Since people are emotional creatures..."

Stories should be told as if they are happening now. Bring the audience with you on the journey so they can feel what you felt, see what you saw, hear what you heard and experience whatever else you experienced.

A popular acronym in the public speaking realm is VAKS, which stands for Visual, Auditory, Kinesthetic and Smell. It's a good checklist to cross reference your stories. You want to give the audience enough information to form a picture, but don't overdo it. Ask yourself as you prepare, does each detail contribute or pull the audience away from your point? When describing something to the audience you want to hit those senses whenever possible. Do it briefly, but powerfully. If you take too long to describe things, the story will lose momentum. Use words that create the strongest image in order to set the scene, describe the environment, give depth to the characters, deepen the mood, or whatever else is relevant to the story.

Here is an example: *I launch myself out of my car and slam the door shut. As I approach the broken-down home I can smell the rotting animal corpse. The wind feels like ice on my skin. The streetlight in front of the house is out, so I use my cell phone to navigate to the front door. The frustration is boiling over in my mind and that son of a bitch is going to pay. I know what I have to do.*

Remember, the audience doesn't get to rewind your speech to go over any details they missed. You have one chance. They either understand or they don't. Make their lives easier by choosing words that are simple and that create a memorable image in their minds.

Don't Skimp on the Dialogue

Dialogue is an incredible tool. It is a fun and powerful part of telling a story. Right away this topic makes me think about how I like to use humor on a daily basis with friends and family. One of the ways I like to begin a little exchange, "He's like..." and then I will throw in some over-the-top dialogue from the dude's perspective in my trumped up scenario.

Dialogue is the conversation that goes on between characters in your story. However, it can also be the conversation that was going on in your head during the actual experience you are recounting to the audience. We typically think of dialogue as actual words being spoken, but what about character body language? Isn't that part of the dialogue, too? We communicate through body language every single day of our lives, so don't forget to incorporate body language — and that includes facial expressions as part of the presentation.

Let's start with how you can use it for the sake of humor. Dialogue is one of the best places to conjure up humor, and the perfect place to use self-deprecating humor. Sure, it would be nice to tell a story where you could do no wrong, but no one wants to listen to that arrogant crap. The audience would rather hear how human you are and how you've experienced the same pratfalls as them. With this in mind, why not give your characters the best zingers or the funniest non-verbal maneuvers?

For example, in a speech I gave I told a story of my bank charging an unexpected service fee to my checking account. The fee was eight dollars but because I only had five dollars in my account, I was immediately overdrawn. So, as the story goes, I call the bank and right off the bat I am expressing myself as a child would during the terrible twos — yelling at the customer service representative about how upset I was, but acting as though she had personally wronged me. Finally, she had the nerve to tell me, "Well maybe you need to be more financially responsible!"

Stepping out of the story for a moment, I followed up with this in an "I can't believe she said that" sort of way, "So not only is she not helping to resolve my issue, she feels compelled to offer me financial advice. And you know what the worst part about that was?" Pausing for a moment, I confessed, "She had a point."

Tell stories where *you* come off as the doofus. We've all got 'em. Show them you're human and you'll receive laughter as your reward. After all, you get to tell the part of the story where you pick yourself up off the ground, and maybe even how you learned a thing or two.

Dialogue can communicate a lot, more than mere in-story character conversations. We agree, it is a great way to bring out humor, but it is also an effective way to draw out emotion — both from the in-story characters that you are portraying and the audience as well.

I've mentioned you can use *self-dialogue*, or the thoughts that were going through your head at the time of the experience that you are now reliving with the audience. This is a great way to convey to the audience what you were feeling during the original encounter.

Were you frustrated? Scared? Nervous? You can flat-out tell the audience what was going through your mind in order to let *them feel* what you were feeling. Be sure to match your voice to your emotions as well as your body language for maximum effect in bringing them to your emotional level.

You can also take dialogue from your story and direct it to your audience. Going back to my example above, I asked the audience a question directly, "And you know what the worst part about that was?" This helps to further invest them into your story which is what you want. You could even say things like, "What would you have done?" or "How could I have done something so stupid?" These small additions can really add up and make your stories much stronger overall.

Think dialogue and consider it well. As you prepare your speech, map out the specific dialogue for each of your characters. That won't be difficult if you're telling a story that happened to you, but you may need to tweak a word or two to make it funnier or more poignant. I've had experiences from a long time ago where I can remember generally what happened and what lessons may have been learned, but it's difficult for me to remember the exact words that were said. No problem, as long as you convey the message that you learned and internalized, there's nothing wrong with that.

I know what you're probably thinking right now. I know because I've been thinking the same thing. Dialogue is cool.

Don't Fear the...Pause

The *pause* says much more than you think. It is also much harder to master than I ever imagined. Humans hate silence. When silence strikes during a conversation, things get awkward real fast. Try it sometime during conversation, when it's your turn to talk, just sit there and pause for about five or six seconds. Or better yet, allow your speaking buddy to break the silence.

And that's just during an everyday conversation. Imagine pausing during a speech; it's a whole other level of awkwardness. Only, it's really *not*. Remember my story about witnessing a speech where the speaker got lost for more than 10 seconds before resuming? It truly wasn't bad at all. If anything, it built up curiosity because I was starting to wonder if it was intentional or not.

I also mentioned in the example that the speaker's 10-second pause didn't even begin after a particularly emotional or powerful sentence or point, which is often the secret to an effective pause. When you attempt to make such a point — one that you really want the audience to feel or think about — stop! Pause. Let the audience absorb it. Let the emotion saturate every piece of their brain before you continue on.

It gives them time to process what you said and gives them time to respond internally. What if you're getting choked up because you're talking about an emotional event in your life? If you pause, the audience is going to feel it and match the emotion, perhaps even tear up. This is okay. You want the audience emotionally involved during your speech.

One of my brothers gave a keynote speech that I helped him prepare. During the concluding portion of his speech he was talking about our parents and how they were a big part of getting him started with his passion. He got choked up for 15 seconds! Fifteen seconds, folks.

You may be thinking: "What an eternity!" But not so. That emotional pause did more for his entire speech than the rest combined. It left an impression and when I finished watching his keynote, that's what stuck with me. I don't think there was a dry eye in the crowd. Yes, that included mine.

It's remarkable that pauses can trigger such emotional response. In comparison to other stories such as losing a home to natural disaster, or even one as serious as losing a loved one, his story was fairly mild. But, it was still able to summon emotion out of the crowd. If he didn't pause to give the audience time to respond to their feelings then it would not have been as powerful. No doubt about it.

Pauses are also a big part of humor. Right after you deliver the funny business, pause. Allow the audience time to laugh, and as the laughter dies out naturally, then continue to speak. Depending on how funny what you say is will determine the length of the pause.

The pause can also build up anticipation for what's coming next. If you tell the audience, "The next thing I tell you will shock you."...........Pause..........And then slap them with it. I'm sure you've heard the cliché "hanging on your every word", well, that's exactly what the audience will be doing if you use the pause effectively.

What about a pause before ever saying a word? Actually, this is a perfect place for one. Just as pausing can build curiosity for your next words and also allow the audience to absorb your last point. Delaying your first remark creates a bit of anticipation and allows the audience to absorb *you*. So, slow down once you've taken control of the stage, pause, smile, and stare out at the audience before speaking. This shows both control and confidence.

Yet, this *can* be overdone. A good rule to follow is to pause three to five seconds before jumping into your presentation. If you pause for too long at this juncture, it may come off as awkward to the audience. In that same contest speech I mentioned earlier, I paused for a whopping nine seconds before I said a word. This is probably too long in most cases, but for my speech there was a purpose. Since the first words were my yelling "I WANT YOU TO LISTEN TO ME AND I WANT YOU TO LISTEN TO ME RIGHT NOW." I wanted to contrast that with my turn to a calmer demeanor. And it did its job.

So many uses for the pause. So worth it. And as Nike's trademark explains, Just Do It.

Emotionally Charge Your Message

The role of emotions is a powerful one. Emotions fuel people's motivation and often drive them to act — or react. Throughout history and right to the present, world leaders and politicians on every side have probed the public consciousness, looking for the right place to supercharge their message. They don't play the *logic game* (though there may be some logic in the discourse), their desire is often to churn emotions.

Yet this is not a call for demagoguery in your speech. That's because emotion can play just as important a role in a half-time pep talk, a call for charitable donations, or a plea to save the endangered carp! You can relay information in an uninspired fashion all you like. If you want to reach the entire body of the audience, not just those already searching for information, find and use the emotional triggers.

In sales, it's popular dogma that people buy on emotion and then later justify the purchasing decision with some logic. The car salesman will say, "The red convertible sports car will have your hair blowing in the wind, and will make you the talk of the town. Oh yeah, it gets good MPG, too." Give me a break. The car may indeed get good MPG but that's not the primary reason we'd buy it. Perhaps that's the justification we'd blather on about it afterwards, but not the real reason we bought it.

You must appeal to the audience's emotions. You have a reason for speaking — some action you want each member of the audience to take. So in order to better persuade them, you'll need/want to reach them on an emotional level.

There is a variety of ways to do this. If you want to inspire people to "save the leprechauns," you'd better have a sad story about them being slaughtered by treasure hunters.

Take a speech by George W. Bush on 10-7-2002 about U.S. policy toward Iraq — known for his reference to the "mushroom cloud" — it's littered with *fear jargon* in order to sway opinion towards a war. The speech utilized an emotional agenda, for he was indeed trying to stir the pot to gain support for...well, the Iraq war. He was appealing to the emotion of fear.

Now, my advice is to stay away from *fear* as a motivator — unless, of course, you have to sell bomb shelters. Yet the point is clear, emotions are a powerful motivator and should be included in your speeches.

Give Them Eye Candy: Visual Aids

I gotta be honest, I'm not a fan of this one. But remember, speeches are for the benefit of the audience, and if the audience finds them enjoyable or helpful, it should be considered as an option. I'm talking about *visual aids*.

Some examples include slides, video clips, graphs, physical props, live demonstrations, paper handouts, flip charts, white boards, and virtually whatever else you can think of that can visually illustrate a point.

There are a multitude of uses for visual aids, but here are a few common ones:

- They can help the audience understand a point you are trying to make. Perhaps it is a complex idea you are describing, a visual aid is a perfect tool to help them comprehend it.
- To help the audience navigate through your speech points. At the start of each sub-topic that you are going to jabber on about, have a slide that gives a clue as to what you'll be talking about.
- To help arouse curiosity. Have something on a table or a stool on stage, but have it covered (or unopened). As you speak, make references to the mystery object. However, don't reveal what is inside of the box until, of course, you're ready to. The Hollywood film producer J.J. Abrams gave a TED Talk that was centered around a "mystery box." Unfortunately, he never opened that sucker up — and the

curiosity eats away at my soul to this day. Thanks for nothing J.J.

- They can be used to entertain. Even if you're not funny, I bet you can find a slide to do your bidding for you. I rarely come across a presentation that doesn't include an attempt at humor, and with good reason. Funny is in style as attention spans are dwindling.
- A visual aid can be used to evoke an emotional response from the audience. One that comes to mind are commercials about sponsoring children in impoverished countries. Sure enough, sprinkled throughout the commercial are pictures of children looking sad and hungry. Whether moral or not, let it be known that it's meant to tug our emotional strings. Effective.
- A cool bonus of these visual helpers is that they can help with memory retention. Just make sure they're interesting.

Of course, there are some parameters if you want these to work for you.

Make sure each is large enough for everyone in the audience to see. If the audience can't see it, it's not doing its job. This includes having them display an adequately large and readable font.

The amount of text on the slides should be minimal – I'm talking three to six words and that's it. A block of text is too much. It takes too long to read and can be overwhelming to the audience. Have plenty of blank space to encourage their viewing each word.

To that end, avoid bright colors like yellow for the text. It's not easy on the eyes. You can't go wrong with white text on dark colored background or black text on a light colored background. It's all about the contrast. If you use a dark slide color, either as a solid color or an image, use white (or close to it) for the text color.

Don't overuse visual aids and allow them to dominate your speech content. You are the main attraction; the visuals are the welcome sign.

Keep them out of sight until you are ready to use them. And when you're done with them, remove them from the audience's view (if possible). It may be confusing if a visual used for a previous point is still flashing on the screen while you're talking about something completely different.

Don't read from the screen. Visuals aren't a substitute for knowing your material although they can help mark your speech course. Rely on preparation instead. If they happen to jog your memory, wonderful.

When you first present a visual, show it to the audience and then pause. Let them see it first before you start talking. If using slides, don't block the screen while speaking. Move off to one side or the other, and better yet, do this before showing the slide.

If you are giving the audience handouts, make sure they aren't looking at them while you are talking. They should be focused on what you are saying. You could use them as a summary, which they can take home and reference later on, or perhaps these can include additional information to back up your main arguments.

You want to avoid passing them out at the beginning because they will be distracting (unless it's done before you're introduced). If you pass them out at any time other than after your presentation, you could ask that they put the handouts under their seats before continuing with your talk.

Worth mentioning again, due to the nature of visual aids, arrive at the venue early and get the technological stuff in order. Make sure everything is working. Bring the necessary cords, adaptors, etc. even if the host says they'll have them. Things get lost, people forget. That's life. Have a backup plan. Perhaps physical props that can replace your slides. In fact, if you're really on your game, be prepared to give your speech without visual aids altogether.

The Inevitable Call to Action

And now we dive into the most important part of the speech — the call to action. It should come during the conclusion of your speech after you've recapped your main points.

The call to action is this: What is it you want your audience to do? What has your entire speech set them up for? What specific, concrete action do you want them to take as a result of hearing your speech? I'm sure these three questions could have easily been condensed into simple question, but by asking three instead of one, I forced you to have to consider the matter a bit more.

And I think you should.

Your call to action should actually be *the very first thing* you decided upon before developing the fullness of your speech — not something you simply throw in as an afterthought. It's the foundation of your speech, of which the balance of your remarks must support this action.

But more than that, your speech should plot a clear course that lays out the benefits the audience will receive for doing what you want them to do. They most definitely should be compensated in some way — even if it's getting a warm fuzzy feeling for contributing to the Save the Squirrels Society. And if you're a supporter, you might also want to plead with members of the Save the Hawks Society.

Let's face it, an audience isn't going to do something just because you say so, *Simon*. Humans tend to be selfish, are easily distracted and selectively charitable. This doesn't mean that they won't help or assist in a cause, but you can't overlook their nature to ask, "What's in it for me?" If you don't fall into this category, I applaud you — *individually*. However, in addressing any collective audience, my advice is to offer them some benefit in exchange for heeding your call. It's safer than hoping they'll respond simply because Simon said.

And because motivation is such a short-lived stimulant, it's in your best interest to have your listeners complete this action *now* — or as close to it is as possible. And to ensure the audience doesn't procrastinate (and ultimately do nothing) you must be specific with your call to action. Don't say, "Help save the squirrels!" That's so broad that you'd paralyze them. Should they start making designated crosswalks so the squirrels don't get plastered to the pavement? If the audience doesn't know the exact steps to take, they won't take any steps. And your squirrel cause could be roadkill.

To combat this, give them the clear "next step." Your directive could be: "You can help today by writing a check for five dollars to the Save the Squirrels Society and dropping it in the jar at the back of the room." That may not be the most glamorous call to action, but at least it's specific and within their power to do it. Or what about this one, and you know what, go ahead and read it in the voice of Morgan Freeman for full effect, "So tonight there's an opportunity to change the fate of the squirrel world. Right now a clipboard is traveling around the room and will land in your lap at any moment. On this clipboard is a petition to create a vast squirrel settlement. This settlement will be used to house the majority of the squirrel population so that they may thrive on this planet free from poverty and sickness — they will even have their own psychiatric ward, too. Please sign it (PAUSE) and save the squirrels." Can you tell I like squirrels?

Here's an important note — the call to action should be both possible and plausible. You wouldn't ask the audience for their unborn children. It's just not going to happen. Yet some calls to action may require more effort or resources from the audience than others, but you must do everything you can to position it right at eye level or arms reach. If you want them to fill out a questionnaire, then designate a small portion of time for them to do this. And not only that, pass out the questionnaires with a pen to each member of the audience. Don't unwittingly provide them any excuses. If there is an available out, such as "Oh, I didn't have a pen," count on it being exercised.

If you have done your best to establish your supporting points building up your call to action, finish strong by making it as clear and easy for the audience to act.

***

These combined segments make up the majority of a speech's content. Not all speeches will have everything we've gone over, but many of these are staples and should be present in your speech in one form or another. The great thing is that you're unique, use these as a guide and don't forget to add your personal touch.

Go over them. And give them plenty of consideration when constructing your next presentation.

CHAPTER 5

PRACTICE: THE DISRESPECTED TREASURE

Just like any other skill you want to become proficient at, you must practice. Not only for a specific speech for which you're preparing, but also for your overall ability as a communicator. Practice refines your speeches and in turn, develops your personality while on stage. Even if you don't have a speech planned, it's important to stay prepared. Be habitually warmed-up and primed for action on a minute's notice because you never know when a spot may need to be filled. Heck, my sister-in-law one time asked me on short notice to call out announcements during my brother's birthday party...can you say "big leagues?"

Of course, there are plenty of ways to practice and even your means of practicing will be fine-tuned to your preferences, weaknesses and to the available moments in your schedule.

This chapter will go over several invaluable practice methods that I've implemented at one point or another, many of which continue to be a part of my practice regimen. "Enough with the introduction already. Get to it!", said Your Thoughts. Fine. Let's get started.

How Do You Look on Camera?

If seeing actually is believing, then you've got to study a video recording of yourself in action. It's an absolute essential when starting out because the film exposes all. Regardless of what you *thought you did*, when you playback the recording you will see what you *actually did*. The video results are without bias and they're not interested in sugarcoating how you perform, they give the raw story.

For example, you'll see your posture, your movement on stage, overused gestures, your facial expressions, your overall energy and any nervous mannerisms. It's those nervous mannerisms that should be targeted for extermination immediately. Off with their heads.

By doing so you are building your foundation for a more competent presence on stage. Often done subconsciously, the camera will catch things such as touching your nose, ear, your clothing, your hair, your face in general, putting your hands in your pockets and just about any other oddity and they will stand out like flaming underwear. The two that tormented me the most were grabbing my left earlobe and stroking my nose — yours may differ — but they're just as malignant.

And just as the video doesn't sugarcoat your performance, *you* must also be honest with yourself. Don't be shy about critiquing yourself because your openness to criticism is the only route to real improvement. There is no other way, the "odd things" you see yourself doing will be noticed — count on it.

I've come across experienced speakers continuing the same nervous mannerisms even after years of speaking. It could be that the fear is deep-seated which I can fully understand, but maybe they just need to see for themselves on video in order to open their minds up to change. It definitely couldn't hurt.

The best place to film yourself is when you are speaking in front of a group of people because that's when all of your nervous mannerisms will rise up and show themselves to you. The people trigger your fear, and your fear summons the nervous mannerisms like a necromancer raises the dead. You want to see everything because if you don't see it, you can't eradicate it.

However, recording yourself in a private setting may be just as important, but for a different reason. This is where you fine tune the fundamentals such as body language, posture, energy, facial expressions, movement, etc. Nervous mannerisms may still shine through in this case if you're camera-shy, yet that just means you can iron them out sooner.

Recording yourself on video is also a good gauge for monitoring your own improvement. Chances are that over time when you tap into your video archives, it could be a rewarding experience — a dramatic before and after.

How Do You Really Sound?

It may have been good enough for Ben Franklin: "Believe none of what you hear, and only half of what you see." But when it comes to your voice, believe it all. You need to record your speech voice in action. You might be thinking, "But doesn't my camera have audio, too?" And you'd be right. It does, but the audio quality is nothing to brag about. There are high end cameras that do pack some serious audio absorption power, but they're the exception. A more realistic option is a small digital recorder. A decent one can be obtained for about a hundred bucks and is worth its weight in decibels (I have no clue what that even means except that it's usually associated with sound).

The reason why you want quality audio is because you want to hear your true voice—what *other people hear* when you speak. How our voice sounds to us is not how it sounds to listeners. It just isn't. I absolutely hated how I sounded when I first heard my recorded voice. It's not that I sounded like Gilbert Gottfried or anything like that. But it was strange (to me) enough that I was embarrassed to hear it. And that is never good for your confidence.

But ultimately, if you want to perfect your voice or tweak it to your liking, you must first hear it. A lot. Get used to how you sound so you can bury any negative thoughts you may have about it. This is where your faithful digital voice recorder comes in handy. It's portable so you can easily carry it on your person or my preferred choice, in your car. The car is a splendid place to record yourself—mainly because of privacy—but also because the time we spend driving is usually wasted time.

If you're someone who drives a lot, think of how much time you have at your disposal that can instead be directed towards something useful. Don't get me wrong, I love jamming to music in my car; however, I try to find a balance. Unfortunately, music isn't going to teach me any new skills or perfect the ones that I'm working on.

So record your voice as often as you can, and go all out doing it. Try saying things in unusual ways and see how they sound. Test your volume, too. Crank up your voice as loud as you can (without actually screaming). Hit the high pitch, low pitch, whatever pitch you can reach, you won't really know until you challenge it. Our voices are tools that can be exercised and strengthened. So hit the gym er, sound studio.

Join a Speaking Club

Perk your attention up for this one, Charlie, because the speech club setting is the Super Bowl of practicing to become a better speaker. It's Toastmasters, baby. This is where you find out who you really are, what demons are inhabiting your mind. This is where you get to know your fears...intimately. And in case you are wondering, the answer is no, I am not being paid to endorse Toastmasters, so you can remove your sales-defense helmet.

It's a no brainer—you have to be part of a speaking club. Toastmasters is the organization I joined, but the important thing is the *belonging*, no matter which one. Whether it's a comedy club, church, school, or whatever, as long as it gives you the opportunity to speak in front of people—preferably people that aren't initially close friends of yours—then it should work fine.

Starting out in a place where you already know everyone provides too much comfort. You need the tension of trying to please or reach an audience who ain't just your grandma. The reason is, family knows and probably adores you. Unfortunately, this means that there just isn't enough "stranger" in the setting to create that nervousness which ultimately translates into growth.

And if you're beginning with a low level of self-confidence or with zero experience in public speaking (as was the case with me) then my suggestion is to join a safe place at first such as Toastmasters. They already have a structure in place for developing communicators. The organization was founded in 1924 so they have had plenty of experience dealing with speakers of all different skill levels. The entire club is focused on *encouraging speakers to grow* rather than discouraging them. By joining a club that takes it easy on you at first, you'll develop a nice layer of rhinoceros skin that will give you a foundation of confidence. From there you can venture out into harsher arenas for further growth.

The problem with getting hit with harsh criticism right out of the gate is that most people will say "Screw it, not worth the pain," and then never return. You might be saying to yourself, "Not me. I can take anything!" And you may be right, but like I noted, this is where you find out who you really are. And that might not happen until you stand face to *faces*.

If you think you are pretty adept already, by all means find a place that will roast you the first time you step to the stage. From my experience though, it's better to be in a more accommodating environment at first.

Joining a club to gain experience and to break down your fears is an absolute essential. There is simply no substitute for a real-life audience. Just join one already.

Off the Cuff?

Speaking *extemporaneously*? Don't worry about it, I hadn't heard of that word either. Maybe these will jog your memory: off the cuff; impromptu; thinking on your feet; ad-lib; improv. You with me now? Good.

This particular form of practice can help you with any type of speaking, be it prepared speeches or impromptu callings. Toastmasters has a portion of each meeting dedicated solely to this, called Table Topics — entertaining to watch but not so easy when it's your turn to deliver. Yet, your "turns" are limited at the club, as you only get a single opportunity per week (depending on how many different clubs you choose to join).

To increase the number of those experiences (and more rapidly improve your level of speech performance) you need to make your own opportunities as in practicing at home, either alone or with a family member or friend serving as your audience.

Furthermore, make it as similar to the Table Topics experience as you can. And make the choices just as arbitrary. Here is what you can do. Get a pack of index cards and on each one write a different word, scenario, emotion, color, etc. Whatever floats your boogie board. Shuffle them up, draw a card, and then go for it. Just start talking about the subject on your card.

It doesn't matter what you come up with. And if you're with a friend or family member, have them draw a card and read the subject out loud. Give it (the topic) a few seconds of thought and then deliver your masterpiece. Feel free to be overdramatic with everything, your voice, your body language, your emotions—all of it while keeping a straight face. In other words, hold back the urge to laugh and break out of character—even if your sole audience member can't.

Let me tell you what this does. Not only do you get the intended benefit of being able to B.S. about anything, but at the same time you develop more control over the other fundamentals of speaking such as your body language, emotional range, vocal variety and stage movement. It's a potent concoction of preparation.

An even more important benefit of developing your impromptu muscle is this. Say you are in the middle of a prepared speech, your mind goes blank and you lose your train of thought. Rather than standing there emotionless, you could jump right into a little bit of impromptu until you remember where you left off. You should, of course, know your topic sufficiently in order to talk about something that relates to your main topic. And a little deviation has got to be better than muttering those hmm'n and umm'n or saying "Now where were we?"

The secret of giving impromptu speeches is to go with your first thought or instinct. Moving your story along beats the heck out of pondering the perfect expression to tell that story. It's better to just commence and branch out from there.

A word of caution though. Make sure your story motif is appropriate for your audience. If you're speaking at an elementary school to children, for example, you might want to refrain from sharing your ideas about eating corpses. I know, it'll be tough, but I believe in you.

After you pronounce your initial thoughts, start talking about things that relate to them—even if your "related" thoughts aren't quite related. You can still find a way to link them. You want it to make sense and not merely arrive as a cluster of jumbled ideas that don't mesh with one another.

Say the topic is about Christmas trees and your first thought is about waking up Christmas morning to open gifts. Perhaps you can branch off and speak about what you'll do with the tree after Christmas.

Example: Waking up to that beautiful pine smelling tree was amazing. With the family gathered around and distributing gifts amongst the ranks, it was always a special day for me as a child. But then it ended and the tree would begin to decay. Was this the last benefit the tree had to offer? I think not. We'd always take that tree out to the hills and have a bonfire. So not only did it offer joy on Christmas, it kept the festivities going even afterwards. It delivered warmth and a good time. Don't give yours up to the trash man, burn that sucker!

There are so many different ways to go on so many topics. But you are unique, so go with what comes to mind for you. Gather from your experiences, put them through your *life lens* (how you see the world) and then put them into words for your audience.

For the last part of your impromptu you want to tie it all together — somehow. You could turn it into a call to action like I did with my example above, or you can simply explain to the audience why it's important. As you practice and develop your impromptu thinking muscle, you will become more elaborate and suddenly making sense of all your crazy thoughts won't be as difficult. And for the record, the bonfire part of my example is completely made up and my family has never once burned a Christmas tree. Admit it, you were already planning the day after Christmas camping trip, weren't ya? Admit it!

Fend Off the Filler Words

Uh, umm, hmm, so...how should I start this? Right. Now you're catching on. Filler words.

Just about everyone has used them at some point. But, there's a problem with them. They dilute your message and can even distract the audience entirely — in the same way nervous mannerisms can.

Filler words include, but are not limited to things such as umm, ahh, uhh, so, like, so like, so like totally bro, ah-err-umm-hmm-lemme think-hrmm-uh-well-like yeah (the most common), and plenty more.

First, what causes them to guest-star in our show of words? The main reasons include nervousness, muddled thinking (lack of clarity), and as I said earlier in the section on pausing, humans *hate* silence. Thus the name, *filler words*.

They fill up what would otherwise be silence. Silence is a beautiful thing, so pipe down and listen up!

How can we get rid of them? Good question. All it takes is a little practice. However, in order to practice removing them from our vocabulary, we must first become aware that we are using them. Do you remember the sections about recording yourself? That is a heck of a way to find out if you're a filler-word practitioner. Joining a Toastmasters club is another splendid way.

In fact, in Toastmasters there's a dedicated "ah-counter" who tallies up exactly how many filler words each speaker uses throughout the meeting. Actually, that's not entirely true — the "ah-counter" stops counting after a paltry 10 filler words. It's like the *mercy rule* in Little League baseball when one team scores so many runs that there's no way the other team can catch up. They can only wait until next game to do better, just like the speaker would need to do at the following meeting. That's the idea anyway.

Okay, now that you've checked the tape and found out that you're guilty, or have met the *mercy rule* in Toastmasters, what next? Shut up. No, not you (at least, not now). I mean *shutting up* is the most effective way to eliminate filler words. Said another way, *pause*. When you feel a *filler* coming on, don't speak.

Such words or sounds offer nothing, so in lieu of them, do nothing — pause. Gather your next thought and then continue on. It's simple. Of course, "simple" doesn't necessarily mean "easy." Although if it were easy, it wouldn't require practice and thus you wouldn't be reading about it in the chapter on practice, right?

Awareness and silence. That's the one-two punch to solving the filler-word riddle.

Faces of the Crowd

Practice in front of a test audience. But it will be a test for you as well as them. My audience of choice is my wife. Did I mention *my* choice? She hates me when it's practice time. The first time she hears me go through it she's interested. But after the fifth time, I'm getting the "Honey, we need time apart" speech in return. My two daughters are good for a minute or so, but usually by then they're storming on stage trying to run between my legs—helpful for building immunity to distractions—but not quite what is needed.

Anyone who sets time aside to hear you could serve as your test audience. And it's not so much to receive feedback, it is so you gain comfort speaking in front of people. Practicing by yourself has its benefits, but when you've got eyeballs locked on you it's an entirely different ballgame. Looking into their eyes can easily distract you, so this is why it's important to practice speaking in front of people—or the equivalent.

I'm talking about audience simulation in the form of a picture. I did a quick search on the internet and found a good one with about thirty people peering at the stage, and of course, the picture was taken from the speaker's vantage point. The audience members all have varied expressions on their faces, but their eyes are clearly visible. It really worked well for me. Perhaps it's that subconsciously a crowd, having all eyes directed towards us, has an effect on us even if they aren't real. If you can't find a test audience, give it a (simulated) shot.

The idea is to become comfortable speaking in front of people, and that requires repetition to train you to focus on your message, even when making eye contact with the members of the audience. Anybody who'll *listen* will do the trick, even if they're two-dimensional on a computer screen.

Meet Your Voice

As a speaker, your voice is your most precious tool. It makes sense, then, to keep it lubricated and primed for action. Previously we addressed experimenting with your voice with the use of recording devices, but this section is more about maintenance and enunciation. Specifically, I am talking about voice exercises.

I've tried a number of set exercises. Some have been surprisingly useful, while others less so or overly technical. Toastmasters International has a resource called "Your Speaking Voice" that goes over breathing and how the voice works, which was extremely educational. It opened my eyes to what I had absolutely no knowledge of—my voice. The resource is a tad bit *academic* but nevertheless my brain was able to embrace some informational bits. Still, no single exercise that I've encountered has been perfect, so after much tinkering around I've developed a process that works for me.

First it's important to learn how to breathe properly. Yes, I really mean it. The difference between chest breathing and belly breathing is distinct. Belly breathing is what you want; chest breathing or *shallow* breathing is what you don't want. The latter provides you with only a limited amount of oxygen; the former fills your tank.

The vocal power comes from your belly. Try this. Rest your hand on your abs just below your sternum. Now take a deep breath. Your hand should have been on an ascending elevator. Now exhale with your hand still there. Your hand should descend now.

What you don't want is your chest and shoulders to rise when pulling in oxygen. They will move slightly regardless, but your belly is what you want to move further outward as you inhale. What's happening is as your lungs fill up with oxygen they push down your diaphragm (I'll just call it belly) which is why your stomach expands. Of course, it's not actually taking in air.

Try this now: Put one hand back to just below your sternum and place your other hand over your chest. Now breathe in as much as you can. And now exhale all the way out. Which hand moved more? It *should be* the one on your belly. If it was the one on your chest, *you've got some practicin' to do.*

I was able to get the hang of this type of breathing by practicing exhaling. But as I would exhale, I would flex my abs and slightly suck in my stomach at the same time. From there I moved on to saying words while exhaling. Another quick test is to say the word "you," but elongate it like "youuu" (not too long though). Do it with no emphasis on your abs and without sucking in air ahead of time. It almost feels like you've emptied out your lungs. Now do the same thing but inhale beforehand and make it a point to flex your abs as you do it. How does that feel? More power maybe?

This breathing technique really helped me get control of my vocal power and an overall control of my voice. I highly recommend it.

A friend of mine is a voice coach and he was offering a speaking voice workshop. I figured it was a valuable opportunity so I signed up. The classes were once a week for six weeks and lasted two hours each. Through the process he taught us how the voice works; how our posture plays a role in our vocal output; the importance of proper breathing; vocal tone; diction; range...ahhhh! Let's just say it was a lot of information, and I mean that in a good way.

We had fun, too. For example, as he was teaching us about the tones of our voice—focus and depth—he explained that focus entailed the power and projection of our voices. Depth, on the other hand, was about warmth and beauty.

The exercise he had us practice (reluctantly at first) was to demonstrate the nasal sound. He had the entire class say "myeah" and "ming" but saying it in the most nasally manner we could muster. We did extended "myeahhhhhhhhhs" and then rapid fire "mings" (ming ming ming ming ming ming ming). Give it a try and you'll see what I mean—it sounds funny. However, it was extraordinarily helpful and the silliness was a small price to pay. The point of the exercise was to demonstrate that the power and projection of our voice originates from the nasal area.

I now use the "myeah" and "ming" technique as an anchor. If I feel my voice is slacking or not finding the power and projection that I want, I'll lash out with some "myeahs" and some "mings." (**WARNING:** *Do this in private. Please don't "ming" or "myeah" during an actual presentation or you'll appear psychotic.*) Instantly when I do this, I find my voice. Never fails.

The depth element of the voice is about the warmth and sincerity of your voice. He explained about the roof of our mouth being rounded, which gives off the distinct sound of beauty. I'll leave the technical explanation to him, but, I will share how to achieve this. It's quite simple, actually. Smile. When you speak with a sincere smile, the warmth comes out naturally. Of course, you must speak more softly or more "warmly" than if you were trying to use power or projection (where you can also smile)—but when it comes to warmth, the smile maneuver sets things.

Warming-Up Your Voice

It's important to warm-up your voice before hammering it with voice exercises and even before a speech. So, grab a glass of refreshing room temperature water and let's get started.

I typically start by humming gently with only a tiny bit of force from my stomach (remember: breathing techniques). I do this three to five times. Here's the process. Each time you hum, first inhale as much as you can and then hum until all the air is exhausted. You'll be surprised at how much air you still have left when you first think you've hummed it all out.

Don't be a hero though. If you're struggling to breathe, stop and suck in some oxygen. And with that, I guess now would be a good time to throw in a disclaimer. If your voice or throat starts to hurt, feel sore, strained, scratchy or some other word that describes a form of discomfort, stop right away. You don't want to do any permanent damage to your golden voice box.

After the initial humming it's time to start loosening up the mouth, jaw, and lips. Yeah, yeah, this isn't exactly a voice warm-up, but it's almost like a first cousin. Trust me, it's related. First open your mouth as wide as possible. Then close it. Now open it again. Repeat this a few times. As you close it, scrunch your lips really tight together as if you were a chimpanzee puckering up for a kiss. (Great image, huh?) But with this additional disclaimer—do this within the privacy of your own home or automobile to preserve a bit of dignity.

Open your mouth and wiggle your jaw from side to side a few times. Don't do it too fast or you could strain your jaw. After that, try rotating your jaw in a circular motion. Even throw in a couple of yawns. The key is to loosen it up in every possible direction so that it's relaxed and ready to use when it's time to speak.

While your lips have received a bit of attention already, now we're going to turn the focus exclusively on them. Extend them. Stretch them. Smile as wide as you can. Pucker up again and *really* squeeze them together. Think: setting the world record for smallest mouth. Now move your *pruney kisser* from the left to the right a few times to really loosen it up. You can even watch an internet video of a chimp. Those fellas know how to make faces.

Now we're going to begin saying words that put emphasis on the lips. Say the following words: mail; movie; coin; mama, we; be

But when you say them, elongate them as much as possible. You also want to exaggerate your lip movement to the extreme. For example, say "moooovieeeee" or "maillllll." Your lips should be separated from your gums as much as possible at the end of saying "mail."

During the voice workshop I told you about earlier, the instructor gave us a phrase to repeat: "Over the lips, the tongue the teeth." Now you say it.

Articulate all the consonants to the best of your ability. Remember, it's not a race, so say it aloud at a slow and exaggerated pace. I tend to get sloppy with my everyday speech and that phrase serves as a reminder to clean it up. The purpose of the exercise was for improving diction, but I find that it works well for my vocal warm-up as well.

Now back to humming. But, this time we're going to do some *power humming*. Start humming softly like you did earlier, however, as you do this put your hand on your throat and massage it. Gently, please — you want to make it to your presentation alive, don't ya? After a minute or two of massaging, stop. Fill your air box up again and start humming as loud and as powerfully as you can.

What's happening is you are letting out more air at once than when you were humming gently, and with more force. You should run out of air sooner, too. Try to power out all of the air from your lungs with each effort. You will know you are doing it right when your lips and teeth are vibrating to the point of a tickle. Do this three to five times and catch your breath in between each repetition.

I do one last exercise after this (not sure if it's just a ritual I've created for myself or what) give a few loud "myeahs" to complete the warm-up. Call me crazy but...you're probably right.

Now, when you finish power humming (and the ritualistic *myeahs*) just talk. Say something. Does your voice feel more resonant? Does it feel louder? I like to describe it as speaking with ease because it feels effortless to speak after doing the warm-up exercises. You should do these exercises daily — or some combination of vocal exercises that work for you — to help strengthen your voice and also before you are actually going to speak. You want your voice to be resonant, so try to warm-up your voice right before you have to speak (or as close to it as *reasonably* possible).

Once you develop your voice, there is simply one less thing to worry about unlike before I took the speaking voice workshop, when I would give entirely too much thought to the likes of: Will my voice crack? Can they hear me? How do I sound? Removing those concerns means my focus can be on more deserving areas such as my message or making a connection with the audience.

Take heed. As silly as some of them are, voice exercises and speech warm-up will improve your speaking voice if you stick to them — don't neglect them.

Practicing Your Speeches

Let's talk about practicing your prepared speeches. Assume that you already have your topic selected, the points that you will talk about dialed in and a call to action in your closing that would raise the dead.

Yet, you should still practice running through your speech. How many times is up to you.

How well do you already know your subject? That is a determining factor. You want to be prepared—and your audience will thank you. Oh yeah, being extremely prepared will also rid you of some of the nervousness that holds back the real you. That alone is worth the price of solid preparation.

Here are the key points. When you practice, go through the entire speech without stopping—particularly if it's a shorter speech of 10 minutes or less. If you make a mistake of any kind, plow right through it until the end. If you constantly stop mid-speech and then restart because of mistakes, you are creating a dangerous habit. It's like priming your awareness to focus only on mistakes. If you should make a mistake, chances are you may lose your train of thought thinking about what you botched. Instead, create the bold habit of continuing on, no matter what mistakes may occur.

There are some practice parameters. Avoid rehearsing your speech too many times in a single day—and especially on the day of your speech. Let it sink in over time. This will be hard if you procrastinate, so try not to do that either.

I've tried running through a speech multiple times (in succession) on the same day that I was to deliver it—and a mental burnout ensued. I was mentally and emotionally exhausted. The damage occurred when I didn't give myself enough time to recuperate any lost energy. I was a sitting duck when it was my turn to speak (with an evaluation that suggested I was almost reading from a script).

Lack of energy can do that. I also lost the edge of excitement for the speech because I rehearsed it too many times in succession. In this instance (having depleted my emotional reserves) I also noticed that nervousness was stronger than normal and more difficult to overcome.

My advice then is to run through your speech no more than three times in any given day and take a break in between, don't machine gun them together. And if you want to solidify your thoughts even more, you can *micro-practice*. Break up your speech into sections and rehearse each section on its own. So, if the body of your speech consists of three main points, practice talking about each point as its own micro-talk. This will be done during the development phase as well, but once it's refined this is an excellent addition to practicing your speech in its entirety. The advice about going through without stopping applies here, too. Don't let screw-ups stop and start you even during these micro-talks (for the same reasons).

The last tip for prepared speeches—try to make it as real as possible. What I mean is to do everything within reason to simulate your speaking environment. Chances are you aren't going to be able to bring in your actual audience, so forget that. But, you can make sure your entire speech is delivered in the manner that you plan on delivering it. That means gesturing for real—*naturally*, of course. It means adding the emotions that you have throughout your speech. If anger is required, get angry. Excitement? Get happy. If you have humorous lines, go ahead and pause as if the audience were laughing. And don't forget to move to where you plan on moving on the stage throughout your speech. Don't half-ass anything.

The added dimension to your practice is putting it *on the clock*. This will get you as close as possible to the actual length of your speech—a critical thing to know. It goes without saying, you need to time yourself during these crucial rehearsals (phone, stopwatch, audio recorder, microwave oven, etc.).

Dramatize Your Emotions

It's hard to get an idea of how much emotion is too much. The simple solution to this is to practice emotionalizing things. The impromptu section earlier on is a good place to implement some dramatic emotions. However, this exercise is slightly different. I'll explain.

Here it is about finding your emotional range by purposely trying to go overboard. Anger, sorrow, excitement—you name it—the goal is to ramp them up and then bring them back down to reality. In doing so, you may find that your initial reality has changed. For example, your emotional output for excitement (that you thought was plenty exciting) may be nearly lifeless to an audience. An attempt at anger might not, it turns out, scare a squirrel (I told you I like squirrels).

Here's the exercise. List emotions on some of those trusty index cards like we did in the section on extemporaneous speaking. Just write something simple like "funny" or "angry."

Similarly, you can also write out scenarios such as: "Funny thing happened right in front of you, you're trying to hold the laughter in, but eventually you can't." It's up to you how elaborate you want to make these—just make sure they involve an emotion.

So, pull out a card, read it and act out the emotion (or emotional scenario). Begin with the emotion you would normally display. Don't think too much about it, just act out the emotion based on your first instinct.

After you finish that, use the same emotion again, only this time take it to the extreme. Push yourself to your Oscar-winning limit. Incorporate all your tools to sell the emotion: your facial expressions, gestures, voice, stage movement—even squeeze out some tears if you can. If you are able to record these sessions you'll develop a great resource for self-evaluation on how you perform each. If you have a friend or family member present, they can help critique your emotional intensity, as well or give other feedback that the video can't.

You may find that your "overboard" version is perfect. Or maybe your first enactment is perfect. Perhaps neither. But, after you see them you will be able to better judge what intensity would be best. That is the point of this exercise. It serves a purpose. Have fun with it.

Seriously, Write It Down

This next form of practice is more than a speaking exercise. It's a life exercise that serves several important functions, some of which also happen to improve your ability as a speaker. Unfortunately, it's an exercise I had to learn the hard way—by failing to do it. That's not, however, my advice to you.

I had heard this advice many times before—from comedians to successful entrepreneurs to spiritualists: Write down the ideas that come to you. So simple. And yet, a technique rarely practiced.

Great ideas come from many sources, some from books, some just click into your head as inspirational thoughts. Others launch from the mouths of children with their wisest or most ridiculous pronouncements or in the quirky experiences you may encounter with friends or strangers, or even from the troubles that confront you on a given day. Your receptacle for these ideas need not be a journal (though it could be) rather something even more mobile that you can carry around with you all the time. After all, you never know when something important will flash into your head or when a life changing experience will appear—or more likely, *disappear.*

The reason I didn't follow this advice *the first hundred times I heard it* was that it was too easy. There was nothing technical about it. It didn't proclaim to be the "long lost cure for salvation that's been buried for thousands of years." Yet, who says an exercise needs to be technical to be effective? Anyway, it took several experiences for me to finally do so, but I learned.

The process went like this. I would get a great idea that inspired me to do something, or rather to *want to do something,* but then life got in the way. I would go to work, plow my normal daily routine, return home and the idea or the perspective I briefly enjoyed just vanished.

You're probably wondering "Well, if it was forgotten then how'd you remember?" Good question. It was only after a month or so later that I would get another idea that reminded me of the idea that previously occupied my mind (but had forgotten). After a few of these experiences I finally realized what I was missing—recall. Once I did remember them, I still didn't write them down *at first,* however I started becoming more aware of the ideas that came and went. This awareness led me to finally start jotting down these important ideas.

Your instructions are pretty straightforward: just write down things that come to you which you feel are important or that have some emotional effect on you. I gave an example earlier in the chapter relative to overcoming fear; here it is again:

There is no such thing as perfect.
It's okay to make mistakes.
If you do make a mistake, don't beat yourself up.
Stop being careful and set yourself free.
Be yourself, trust yourself.
Enjoy the journey.

That little note still plays an integral role in my life.

Vital to your note-taking is that they must have enough detail for you to recall where your mind was at the moment. If too brief, the notes leave too much to after-the-fact interpretation. You don't want that given you felt it was important enough to write it down. Being too sparse with words, has let a few ideas slip through the cracks.

Also, be especially careful of letting too much time pass before you go back and read over your notes. There have been times, because of this time lapse, when I couldn't even remember writing down certain notes, let alone what the idea once meant to me. Sure, there's a chance that a different interpretation leads you to a new and better idea, but I'd prefer not to take a chance. Get that sucker down on paper. Write that thought clearly enough that you will be able to immediately remember how it made you think or feel, and re-read it soon after to internalize its context.

If the thought or idea is a quotation or a passage from a book, write it down word for word — or the same message in your own words. These are for your own personal reflection and don't necessarily require annotation, still you might note the source as a guide to cross-referencing or further clarification. If it's not an abstract thought or idea, like an event or a funny experience, you can get away with putting a word or two which you can use as a *tickler* — just enough to jog your memory. This is because personal experiences are easier to remember than frames of mind.

Here are the benefits of this exercise:

- It helps you work through the ideas clearly.
- Provides you with topics to speak about.
- Allows you to record "mental breakthroughs" that build confidence within you. The added benefit to

this is that you can look at them again and again when you need an extra boost.

It takes awareness. It requires forming the habit. It takes writing down your thoughts and impressions. It takes reviewing what you have written. I realize it's a bit of work. I accept the fact you may be slow to apply it for the same reasons I didn't. Maybe it's one of those things that requires learning the hard way.

I respect that, just know that it's played an important role in my life—and it damn sure can for you, too.

Focused Practice

This following exercise helps you focus on specific areas you want to improve. Before your next speech day, write down one or two things that you want to improve on.

Perhaps you wandered too much in your previous speech, or maybe your stage fright was near paralyzing. You'll want to improve on those this time around, so jot them down on a sticky note and after you give your speech, go back to the note and give yourself a letter grade (A, B-, C+, etc.). It's important not to list too many things, I personally prefer one or two at the most. And try not to think too much about them during your presentation, although you want to be conscious of them so you can improve.

When it comes time to grade, be brutally honest with yourself. But, don't get down on yourself if you grade yourself low. That just means you know where you need to improve which is valuable information.

It's a simple way to iron out bad habits—just don't show the report card to Mommy.

Monitor Yourself

Like the previous exercise, this next one involves speech day. It's not so much an exercise, but rather a focus on self-awareness. On speech day, both before and after you speak, pay attention to your thoughts, emotions and any physical sensations (hunger and energy level).

Before you speak the checklist looks like this: How do you feel? What are your thoughts focused on? Are you trying anything new this time in terms of preparation? Are you relaxed or are your nerves taking a grip on your confidence? Are you tired or full of energy? You can reflect on these questions throughout the entire day—not just in the small window of time before you speak.

After you speak record these: How do you feel? Is your energy level completely wiped out? Was your mouth dry making it difficult to speak? Are you beating yourself up for making a mistake during your speech? Were you able to corral your nervousness easier than your past performance(s)? Did any new method of preparation work? Run your mind through the entire speech and search for the answers to these questions. The answers will give you a mountain of information that you can use for next time.

Awareness of these things allows you to examine "the experiment" that is your speaking effort. You are implementing small changes to your mental focus and monitoring the results. Ultimately, you want to determine what is working and what is not. Then, based on these changes, you will slowly be able to get better control of your thoughts and emotions. It is here you will slowly develop a system that works for you—from what you eat beforehand, to what you do and think about in order to maintain your composure. And even how you treat yourself afterwards.

Like yellow in a toilet or mines in a mine field, you cannot dismiss the above elements to randomness. They are present and they are going to control you if you do not address them.

It takes an intentional focus to listen to yourself and your body particularly when nervousness shoots up. It's not easy to do. However, if you do, you will take giant strides toward wiping out your speech jitters. And that's a worthy goal.

You want perfection, right? Well, I want to fly like Superman. Perfection in public speaking is equally elusive, I'm afraid. But, what you can do is continually strive to get as close to perfect as possible. And to do that: Practice. Practice. And then practice some more. This is where you will refine your skills in order to become an able communicator. Practicing will help you implement and solidify good habits — the fundamentals of public speaking.

We went over several methods of practice, but don't feel overwhelmed. You don't have to do them all, all of the time. Play around with some of them and see if they resonate with you. After all, you are preparing yourself, transforming yourself, it only makes sense to do what works for you.

A good idea would be to actually schedule a time for you to practice. The most important thing though, is to practice. Something. Anything. Schedules are busy, I understand. We're all busy. But even for just a couple minutes a day. Say you're filling up at the gas station and you're just standing there, why not practice putting your hands at your side, and keeping them there. You might notice the urge to fiddle around with your hands, put them in your pocket, fold your arms, play with your keys, etc. That's actually one of my favorite exercises to do. It's simple and plus, I don't have anything better to do except watch the gas pump meter calculate next month's credit card bill.

There are opportunities to practice all over the place. You just have to put in a little effort and be alert enough to see one.

Dig in.

CONCLUSION

IS IT REALLY OVER?

Wow. We're almost done. Not quite though, so stay with me as we lean toward the finish line.

It's important for you to be able to share your ideas and your passions as perfectly as you are able. You won't be satisfied, otherwise. I've done my best to show you my journey and what I've learned in hopes to fill in the hidden links — the things I wish I had known before leaping into what some might call, torture.

Sadly though, I think I may have told too much. And I don't mean my own embarrassing thoughts or experiences because those are actually gifts and the seeds, which motivated me to write this book. Rather my reservations refer to the insights that came as a direct result of my internal struggles, my self-subjection to pain. Would it have been better to let you experience them on your own? I don't know. I do know that they were so damn meaningful to me that I couldn't resist sharing, and I sincerely hope that they help you.

It's clear that you are interested in breaking free from your own personal barriers, your own self-imposed (or self-accepted) perfectionist limitations. Or maybe you just want to communicate better. I began my journey simply to learn how to become a better communicator. I wasn't looking at it from a standpoint of personal growth, but that's certainly what I found. I believe it's what you will find, too.

Believe in yourself. Believe in your importance. Believe in what you have to say. If you're a perfectionist like me, then public speaking can provide a pathway and an outlet for that belief. Allow yourself room for mistakes, learn from them and continue on.

A REQUEST LACKING SHAME

(Shameless usage of my daughters)

Thank You For Reading My Book!

I mean it, thanks for taking a chance on my book. I know how many other books there are to choose from, so it truly means a lot to me.

Your input is important to me. I shamelessly ask that you please spare a few minutes of your time to leave me a helpful review on Amazon letting me know what you thought of the book.

Yes, I'd love a nice review but if you want to lay the smack down, that works too. This truly is the lifeblood of books — feedback from real people, from you.

Thanks so much for your help!

~ Matt Kramer

REFERENCES

CHAPTER 2: Overcoming Mental Obstacles

Chapter 2 Introduction:
"There are only two types of speakers, those that are nervous and those that are liars." - Generally attributed to Mark Twain - Origin unknown.

Trust Yourself:
Ruiz, Miguel. "Chapter 3: The Second Agreement." *The Four Agreements: A Practical Guide to Personal Freedom*. San Rafael, CA: Amber-Allen Pub., 1997. N. pag. Print.

Capture What Inspires You:
"Home - GSTV." *GSTV*. N.p., n.d. Web. Jan.-Feb. 2015. <http://www.gstv.com/>

Controlling The Fear:
Lieberman, M. D., N. I. Eisenberger, M. J. Crockett, S. M. Tom, J. H. Pfeifer, & B. M. Way. "Putting feelings into words: Affect labeling disrupts amygdala activity in response to affective stimuli." Psychological Science 18, no. 5 (2007): 421-28 <http://www.scn.ucla.edu/pdf/AL(2007).pdf>.

Controlling The Fear:
"Limbic System: Amygdala (Section 4, Chapter 6) Neuroscience Online: An Electronic Textbook for the Neurosciences | Department of Neurobiology and Anatomy - The University of Texas Medical School at Houston." *Limbic System: Amygdala (Section 4, Chapter 6) Neuroscience Online: An Electronic Textbook for*

the Neurosciences | Department of Neurobiology and Anatomy - The University of Texas Medical School at Houston. University of Texas Medical School at Houston, 1997. Web. 12 June 2015. <http://neuroscience.uth.tmc.edu/s4/chapter06.html>.

CHAPTER 3: Bathe In The Fundamentals

Show Some Teeth:

"2014 California International Trade Show and Business Plan Competition Recap | Virtual Enterprises International." *Virtual Enterprises International 2014 California International Trade Show and Business Plan Competition Recap Comments.* N.p., 13 Jan. 2015. Web. 05 Dec. 2014. <https://veinternational.org/blog/2014-california-international-trade-show-business-plan-competition-recap/>

CHAPTER 4: The Blood And Guts: Speech Content

Do You Remember Now:

Wikipedia. Wikimedia Foundation, n.d. Web. 15 Feb. 2015. <http://en.wikipedia.org/wiki/Method_of_loci>.

Do You Remember Now:

"Welcome to the Worldwide Mind Sport of Memory - The World Memory Championships." *The World Memory Championships.* N.p., n.d. Web. 02 Apr. 2015. <http://www.worldmemorychampionships.com/>.

Do You Remember Now:

"Our Organization | About | TED." *Our Organization | About | TED.* N.p., n.d. Web. 11 Feb. 2015. <https://www.ted.com/about/our-organization>.

Do You Remember Now:
TEDTalks: Joshua Foer--Feats of Memory Anyone Can Do. TED, 2012.
Online Video. <http://www.ted.com/talks/joshua_foer_feats_of_
memory_anyone_can_do?language=en>.

Add A Little Humor To Your Life:
Nielsen, Leslie, Priscilla B. Presley, George Kennedy, Robert K.
Weiss, and David Zucker. *The Naked Gun: From the Files of Police
Squad.* Hollywood, CA: Paramount, 1988.

Shock 'Em Dead:
Redd, Nola Taylor. "How Fast Does Light Travel? | The Speed of
Light | Space.com." *Space.com.* N.p., 22 May 2012. Web. 10 Mar.
2015. <http://www.space.com/15830-light-speed.html>.

Tie Your Main Points To Something:
Les Brown speech. "Achieve The Dream In 2015." Renaissance
Village. Moreno Valley, California. January 15, 2015.

Transition Through The Journey:
Valentine, Craig. *Transition Teasers.* Rep. N.p., 2009. Web. 23 Oct.
2014. Pages 2-3 <http://www.52speakingtips.com/>.

Emotionally Charge Your Message:
U.S. Policy Toward Iraq. Perf. George W. Bush. C-SPAN, 7 Oct. 2002. Web.
<http://www.c-span.org/video/?173041-1/us-policy-toward-iraq>.

Give Them Eye Candy: Visual Aids:
"Visual Aids." *Visual Aids.* University of Alabama School of
Medicine - UAB, n.d. Web. 11 Nov. 2014.
<http://www.uab.edu/uasomume/fd2/visuals/page2.htm>.

Give Them Eye Candy: Visual Aids:
Tedtalks: J. J. Abrams-the Mystery Box. TED, 2008. Online Video. <http://www.ted.com/talks/j_j_abrams_mystery_box?language=en#t-302076>.

CHAPTER 5: Practice: The Disrespected Treasure

Audio Record Yourself:
"Believe none of what you hear, and only half of what you see." Generally attributed to Ben Franklin - Origin unknown.

Join A Speaking Club:
The first meeting was held at the YMCA building on October 22, 1924. "Toastmasters History." *Toastmasters International*. N.p., n.d. Web. 27 May 2015. <http://www.toastmasters.org/About/History>.

Getting To Know Your Voice:
Your Speaking Voice. Rep. no. Rev. 6/2011- Item 199. Toastmasters International, n.d. Web. 23 Mar. 2014. <http://www.toastmasters.org/~/media/B7D5C3F93FC3439589BCBF5DBF521132.ashx>.

ACKNOWLEDGEMENTS

No one gets very far down the path without support, so here I offer thanks. Thank you to the souls who have helped me throughout my journey. Thank you to those that are aware they've helped, and even those that have no clue. My wife Cindy who has served as the best single audience member ever, I appreciate your patience, your love, and your continued support. Thanks as well to my daughters Brooke and Jacelyn for helping me keep life in perspective, I am indebted to you both for all your laughter that has filled my heart.

To my Dad, George Kramer, an author himself (and Fresh Water Fishing Hall of Famer) who continues to be an inspiration in that he lives his life doing what he loves. Oh yeah, he helped edit the crap out of this book, too. Thank you for the many conversations about the writing process, without them I'd have been spinning my tires to the rims, trying to finish this book. Thank you, to my Mom, Diana Kramer, for carrying me into this world and putting up with me over the years. Thank you to all my eight siblings, starting from eldest to youngest, Garaghty, Blythe, Jared, Lynsey, Adam, Kary, Andrew, and Michael — I'd be second to last. I can't thank you all enough for all the perspectives you've provided me growing up which have been invaluable. The many fond memories we share bring countless half-circles (lower half) to my mouth.

An extra thanks to my brother, friend, and boss, Andrew Kramer for giving me work that has allowed me to provide for my family and for being there to help out during some rough times in my life.

To my life-long friend Jeremy Randall, that no matter how much time passes that we haven't seen each other, we always pick back up like it was just yesterday, I am grateful as well.

Additionally I send thanks all the incredible people that I've met through Toastmasters and the experiences we've shared that have helped shape this book. To my friend, Norm Boaz, who helped me find and use my voice, which was apparently buried deep within me. A special thanks to my accountability buddies Rémi Malahieude and Suzanne Berkey who offered me valuable feedback, support, and motivation during the book writing process and especially down the stretch when "almost done" turned into "not even close."

To friend and design master, Tino Hertz, who helped countless times with the book design—thanks buddy! And there's no way I could forget friend and voiceover extraordinaire, Gary Johnson. I am thankful for your time and attention to detail in constructing the audiobook.

To the many squirrels that have crossed my path leading me to believe that they were funny enough to add to this body of text. I salute you.

Thanks as well to all of the authors out there whose books and content have provided me with many insights and motivations. You've made unending education possible for everyone who desires to learn.

And finally, thank you to the lovely energy source that we call life. I am grateful for the opportunity I've been given to experience it and the free will to live it how I choose.

ABOUT THE AUTHOR

Matt Kramer has not been interviewed on Fox or CNBC, nor has he trained the corporate staff of a Fortune 500 company. And no, you're not going to view the "As Seen on TV" logo on his website. Frankly, he learned the art of public speaking in a most excruciating way, solo, without a mentor to guide him every step of the way. He's pushed through his own fears and pain to deliver you his heart and soul in this book. He doesn't claim to be "professional" speaker or guru. He's about *real help*, not real hype.

Kramer went from being terrified of merely standing in front of an audience to speaking competitively in the 2015 Toastmasters International Speech Contest. There he captured first place at three different levels before bowing out at the district contest.

He was as surprised as anyone, given the path he negotiated. In particular, the fear he had encountered through public speaking was so intense, for the first seven months it didn't subside — not even an inch, he related. However, his eventual breakthrough in overcoming the fear is what solidified his passion for speaking and has driven him to share what he's learned.

As a part of that effort, he also launched his company, Tactical Talks, to help others overcome the fear of public speaking and, in the process, help them build the confidence to go after their individual passion. Kramer also provides coaching to help ensure that presentations, as he put it, "suck *less*." On his blog he provides tips on how to overcome "stage fright" and become a better communicator as well.

Says Kramer, "Check out the blog after you've read this book front to back!"

Sure thing Matt, sure thing.

www.tacticaltalks.com/blog

Proof

Made in the USA
Charleston, SC
10 December 2015